Secrets from a Chinese Kitchen

SECRETS FROM A
CHINESE
KITCHEN

VIVIENNE & JENNY LO

PAVILION

Dedication

This book is dedicated to mother for all her hard work stoking the Rayburn. Thanks are due to Victoria Conran for her natural enthusiasm and clarity; to Tim Gordon for his recipe testing and to everyone at the Traditional Acupuncture Centre next door for their insatiable appetites.

First published in Great Britain in 2000 by
PAVILION BOOKS LIMITED
London House, Great Eastern Wharf
Parkgate Road, London SW11 4NQ
www.pavilionbooks.co.uk

Text © Vivienne and Jenny Lo
Photography © Ian Wallace
Design and layout © Pavilion Books Ltd.

Text designed by Andrew Barron & Collis Clements Associates

A CIP catalogue record for this book is available
from the British Library.

ISBN 1 86205 366 9

Set in Swiss 721 light and Palatino
Printed at BookPrint, S.L. in Spain
Originated by Anglia Graphics in Bedford

10 9 8 7 6 5 4 3 2 1

This book can be ordered direct from the publisher. Please contact
the Marketing Department. But try your bookshop first.

Contents

A secret journey

The greatest secret is that food can take you home wherever you are: it gives you a sense of identity. Whether it is Peking duck and pancakes or dimsum, if you know your food, you know where you are in the world.

Father trained well for his work as a restaurant inspector, a cookery writer and restaurateur. From Fuzhou to Beijing, Berlin to Manchester, wherever the best food was to be had, he was there – making memories out of every meal. Throughout the post-revolutionary decades, he was completely cut off from his family in Southern China, but he could still savour his earliest, most deep-rooted memories. He could, in a sense, eat his way home.

The secrets father taught us do not revolve around the kitchen stove, but around the appreciation of fine food – he was a gourmet in the most glorious, catholic sense of the word. By the time we left home we had taken thousands of gourmet trips round China, without even setting foot on its soil.

We knew the North China plains, bordered by mountains to the north and stretching away in the west to the borders of Inner Mongolia. The plains are unsuitable for rice-growing, so the North is the land of wheat cultivation – for noodles, steamed buns and dumplings. Northerners like to eat plain-cooked meats, their sauces flavoured with leeks, onions and garlic. Mutton and lamb, the meat of the nomadic people to the north and north west, are much more popular here than in the south. As children we often celebrated major events round a steaming Mongolian hot pot full of broth in which we cooked lean lamb, prawns and vegetables, served with piquant sesame dips.

Eastern Chinese cuisine focuses on Shanghai and the fertile areas surrounding the Yangzi delta, the great rice-producing lands. Before the revolution, Shanghai was a playground for rich Chinese and father would tell us of lavish banquets redolent with the colour of pink lobsters, steamed fish and rich, fresh stir-fried vegetables.

Further south the flavours of Canton are the West's most visible representatives of Chinese culinary traditions. Fish and seafood are, unusually, often combined with meat; cooking methods – poaching and steaming – preserve natural flavour. From Canton come dimsum, steamed and deep-fried snacks, on the menu from mid morning.

Inland towards the sources of the Yangzi, is land-locked Sichuan, China's largest, most fertile and most densely populated province. Sichuan cooking's characteristic flavour comes from the ruddy *hujiao* (Sichuan peppercorn) which at first, deceptively mild, suddenly explodes its heat. Another famous style of Sichuan cooking is *yuxiang* (fish fragrance). Some people say it is a term used for dishes spiced with red-brown hot bean sauce and a touch of sweet and sour; others say it refers to the combination of spring onions (scallions), ginger and soy. For us the flavours of Sichuan were learnt during their wave of popularity in the West during the 1970s and 1980s.

When we were growing up, our basic problem was that, although our palates were finely tuned to appreciate quality and to detect individual ingredients, we were kept out of the kitchen. So as soon as we left home, we had to learn everything from scratch. Much of my adult life has been spent recreating the taste of childhood and cooking for my family of six, adapting recipes to suit the foibles of the next generation of British-born children. I have travelled extensively in China and have grown to love the cooking of Sichuan, Canton and Beijing, laterly I have also developed an interest in cooking for health and the tradition of combining food and herbs.

Jenny, on the other hand, has spent her whole life in the food business. She ran the first Memories of China and Ken Lo's Kitchen, the Chinese cookery school, when she worked with with a host of well-known chefs.

Nowadays, the Teahouse, our café on London's Eccleston Street, is a haven for anyone who wants basic, fresh Chinese food without pomp or waiting more than 15 minutes. We have learnt to cook out of necessity, to enrich our own lives and those of our family and customers. But our experience has convinced us that there are not so many secrets to learn in order to prepare good, well-balanced regional dishes. The best of Chinese food can be narrowed down to a few simple and distinctive styles, outlined in the chapters of this book, where we explain the art of hehuo, harmonising the heat, and correctly combining foods and spices.

These recipes have been taken from our previous collections, but retested and improved for the European cook. Victoria Conran – chef, acupuncturist, medical anthropologist and veteran biker, in no particular order – has spent many hours stir-frying and making excellent suggestions for modifying each dish. Many recipes are also new to us, tried and tested during recent research trips to Northern China. The rest have been given to us by friends and family.

If we have a culinary mission, it is to distil the spirit of essential Chinese cookery, while remaining sensitive and responsive to changing trends and the ingredients available in the West. We therefore invite you to follow us on our own secret journey, a journey that is, in a sense outside of a time or place, and one that will transport the myriad of flavours of China, 'The Middle Kingdom', into your own home.

Special Ingredients

Balachan
Fermented shrimp paste responsible for the delicate seafood flavour in Malaysian and South Sea spice paste and dips.

Bak choy
Chinese greens with a small rounded leaf and bulbous white base. The word bak choy is Cantonese for *bai cai* or Chinese leaves.

Bamboo shoots
Ivory shoots of bamboo available in cans, sliced or cubed. They add texture to stir fries. Store, covered with water, in the refrigerator.

Beans and bean pastes
Black bean (salted black beans)
This tiny but potent bean must be chopped and soaked in hot water for 10 minutes before use. Use sparingly, especially when soy sauce is added. Its salty savouriness complements the fresh taste of seafood particularly well.
Firm bean curd
Type of bean curd generally referred to in our recipes. Also available dried in sheets.
Red fermented bean curd (red bean cheese)
A red smooth substance available in jars or cans. Cubes of bean curd are fermented in red wine, rice wine and salt. Available red or white, the red version is extremely pungent – It is good as a marinade or for sauces.
Red (aduki) bean paste
Small beans, sweetened and puréed for soups, cakes and puddings.
Silken bean curd
A softer version of firm bean curd, which can be eaten raw or added to a clear soup stock. (it falls apart in stir fries.)
Yellow bean paste
Available as the cooked bean itself, or in sauce form, it has a strong salty flavour, ideal for marinades or slow-cooked dishes.

Chestnuts (dried)
Soak them for 1 hour in boiling water, then simmer for a further hour. Added to slow-cooked meats, to give a natural sweet and dry taste.

Chillies
Green chillies are sweet and milder; the longer, thinner and more wrinkled red ones get, the hotter they become.

Chinese chives (*jui cai*)
An aromatic, pungent flavoured vegetable. Chopped finely and added to the stuffing for dumplings, or stir-fried with vegetables, they are unforgettable.

Chinese dried mushrooms
You can do anything to these black, thick-capped fungi and they won't fall apart. Braised or slow-cooked, they adopt an earthy flavour.

Chinese cabbage
Known simply as 'white vegetable' in China, they have a large light green leaf and broad white centre. They appear in almost every meal in Northern China.

Chinese white radish (daikon or mooli)
This long, white carrot-shaped vegetable is very versatile and tasty – it can be sliced and tossed in sesame for a salad and makes an excellent stock base.

Dang gui
Chinese angelica, one of the most commonly prescribed Chinese herbs, is thought to act on the kidneys and is especially good for gynaecological problems. It is often combined with lamb or chicken.

Dried shrimps
Widely used to flavour vegetables, savoury dishes and soup. Soak them in warm water for at least 30 minutes before using.

Fish sauce
A thin, translucent brown liquid made from fermented fish that gives a tart saltiness to food. Its use in Thai, Vietnamese and Philippine cuisine is comparable to the use of soy sauce in China.

Five spice
A strong combination of star anise, fennel seeds, cloves, cinnamon and ginger and/or Sichuan peppercorns, used in marinating and cooking. Buy it whole or ground - but use sparingly!

Ginger
Fresh root ginger is essential to Chinese cookery. Choose pieces that are uniformly pale-skinned, firm and round. Ginger juice can be made by mincing the ginger then storing it in the refrigerator.

Golden needles
Dried tiger lily buds, these should be soaked and knobbly bits removed before stir frying.

Hoisin (barbecue) sauce
A thick sauce combining soy with flour, garlic, chilli, vinegar, sesame and sugar. Commonly used in marinades and stir fries. Mixed with peanut butter and sesame oil, it makes a good dip.

Hot bean paste or sauce (douban jiang)
A delicious combination of yellow and black bean with garlic, sesame and lots of chilli it is widely available. A must for stir fries.

Huang qi (radix astragali)
A root commonly used as a tonic and to strengthen the body's defences against infection.

Kelp
A source of iodine, kelp is a seaweed common to Europe and China.

Lotus leaves and root
The large round leaves of the lotus flower, greeny-brown in colour, give an aromatic flavour to steamed rice, poultry or pork. Soak in warm water before using. The dried version has to be reconstituted by soaking overnight and boiling for at least 1 hour.

Millet
There are many different kinds of millet. For congee, use the round, yellow-grained millet commonly available in healthfood shops.

Mung beans
Sprouted for beansprouts, they can be bought as fensi (glass noodles).

Oils
red chilli oil
A few drops of this hot oil, similar to Tabasco, will liven up stir-fries.
sesame oil
One of the most recognisable flavours in Chinese cookery, a few drops in the final stir adds a nutty flavour.
peanut oil
The traditional choice for stir frying, it gives a nuttier taste than vegetable oil, but should be avoided by anyone with a peanut allergy.

Preserved cabbage (snow pickle)
Salty pickled greens sold in cans. We griddle it in oil and use it to garnish soups and poached food.

Preserved duck eggs (*pi dan*)
The shell is a delicate green; inside, the white of the egg is translucent green-black, the yolk just hard. Formerly known as 1000-year-old eggs, they do, in fact, take just days to preserve.

Red dates
Cultivated in neolithic times, these are used in sweet soups and congees and to flavour casseroles. Red dates are thought to enrich the blood and calm the heart. Sweet plums can be used instead, but they don't hold their shape.

Rock sugar
A pure, crystal cane sugar, which has to be ground in a pestle and mortar. Used to thicken and glaze sauces.

Sesame paste
Ground roasted sesame seeds in paste form can be mixed with stock, soy sauce or water. Tahini can be used instead.
Sesame seeds (black or white)
White sesame seeds are toasted or eaten raw. Black sesame seeds are often ground and cooked as a soup, thought to nourish the liver and kidneys.

Shaoxing wine
A famous brand of cooking rice wine, commonly used in stir frying. You can use medium dry sherry instead.

Sichuan peppercorns
Strong and fragrant peppercorns native to Sichuan. Dry-roast them in a wok until the aroma is released and the peppercorns turn brown, then grind in a mortar and pestle.

Sichuan pickle (*zha cai*)
Preserved knobs that grow on the stems of mustard greens. First preserved in brine then chilli pepper it becomes hot and peppery; finely minced it will pep up a stew or stock.

Soy sauce
A staple of the Chinese kitchen, made from fermented soy beans, wheat, yeast, salt and sugar.

Star anise
A dried star-shaped spice native to South China. It has a strong aniseed taste and is best in slow-cooked dishes.

Tangerine peel (dried)
Gives a strong citrus flavour to meats and stews. Soak for 20 minutes in warm water before using, then discard.

Thai mint
Hard to find, yet with a sharp minty flavour. Use basil as an alternative.

Vinegar
Chinese red vinegar is mild and often used in dips; white is useful for pickling. European equivalents can be used instead.

Water chestnuts
Available peeled and canned, they have a crisp white flesh, which adds texture. Fresh water chestnuts are less readily available.

White fungus
Has a sponge-like texture and brilliant white colour. It is often an alternative to snow fungus, which is the gland of the Northern snow frog.

Wind-dried sausage
These salami-type sausages are made either from pork or pork and duck liver. Both should be steamed for 10 minutes before adding to stuffing or other mixed dishes. You can also eat them with rice.

Winter pickle
The most common is Tianjin winter pickle, minced cabbage preserved in salt and garlic. Use it to stuff steamed or roasted meats and fish.

Wood ear (black fungus)
One of the grey-black curly things you've never been able to identify in your soup! It is almost flavourless, but retains its crunchiness after cooking.

Zhengjiang vinegar
Similar to red wine or even balsamic vinegar, it is made from glutinous rice and has a much stronger flavour than rice vinegar.

Stir Frying

The secrets of stir frying

Stir fry is the quintessential fast food. There are many regional traditions, but the basic technique is always the same – to cook quickly, capturing the heat of an intense flame inside the wok. As well as controlling and harmonising the heat (*hehuo*), a basic skill of wok cookery is in blending flavours: rancid, bitter, sweet and pungent.

Not only do stir fry techniques have the virtue of enhancing flavour, but they also retain the natural crispness of vegetables while brightening the colours. If a dish has this quality it is *cui*. Usually there is one dominant ingredient (meat or fish). Secondary ingredients embellish this and bring out its colours, texture and flavour, but the overall effect should be of contrast.

The recipes in this chapter are representative of different techniques. Some use plenty of oil and deep-fry the raw meat and fish first for a few seconds. Vegetables are then stir fried separately and, finally, the meat is returned to the pan. Other styles just throw everything in in stages, using less oil. Marinating adds other variations. There are three basic stages to successful stir frying:

1 Preparation
Cube, slice or mince lean meat finely, cutting against the grain. Vegetables should be cut according to their shape and cooking time (very hard ones may need blanching first). Some meats need to be marinated in soy sauce, garlic, ginger, rice wine, sugar or salt. If you have marinaded the meat, deep-fry it for a few seconds before beginning the main stir fry.

2 The Stir Fry
Make sure all the ingredients are prepared and close at hand. To save time, you can combine ingredients that have to be added together. Use a bland oil such as soy, sunflower, vegetable or peanut. First heat the pan until it will sizzle away a drop of water. Pour in a little oil, swirling it around to coat most of the surface. When it is almost smoking, scatter the vegetables into the pan. Then, turn and flip the food in generous sweeping motions to prevent burning and ensure even cooking. After a few seconds, add all the seasoning and flavourings, plus pre-cooked noodles if using. Bring back to the boil, then turn the heat down and cover. This stage continues for just a few seconds – the aim is to reduce the liquid in the wok.

3 Finishing
Coriander (cilantro), julienned cucumber or finely sliced spring onions bring life to the colour of the dish and add a fresh taste, while a few drops of sesame oil glaze and add flavour. Serve stir fried dishes as soon as possible after cooking.

Lamb with Spring Onions (Scallions)

This is a classic Northern dish and, as is the case with most classics, people argue about the best way of making it. Some say there should be very little seasoning – if the lamb is fresh and thinly sliced, you only need salt. Others say that garlic shouldn't be matched with lamb. At the other extreme there are version's that add yellow bean or oyster sauce. This recipe is at the simpler end of the spectrum and aims for a clean taste. We like the addition of ginger and garlic, which are used liberally.

Slice the lamb into wafer-thin pieces (see Our Secrets). Sprinkle with salt and marinate in 1 tablespoon oil and the *Shaoxing* wine for 30 minutes. Combine the soy sauces, chilli sauce or hot bean paste, vinegar, sugar and pepper.

Heat the wok, then add the remaining oil until it starts to smoke. Add the lamb, ginger and garlic. Stir fry for 10 seconds, then reduce the heat, still turning the lamb in the oil until it changes colour. Immediately discard as much of the oil as possible.

Scatter in the spring onions and toss with the meat. Pour in the soy sauce mixture and turn up the heat as high as possible, turning together for 20 seconds. Add the sesame oil and stock and stir for a further 10 seconds. Serve immediately on a bed of rice.

Serves 2

240 g/8 oz/1 cup lean lamb (eg, neck end fillet)

pinch of salt

4 tbsp vegetable or peanut oil

½ tbsp *Shaoxing* (rice) wine or medium sherry

½ tbsp dark soy sauce

½ tbsp light soy sauce

½ tsp chilli sauce or hot bean paste

½ tbsp *Zhengjiang*, red wine or balsamic vinegar

2 tsp rock or granulated sugar

pinch of freshly ground pepper

4 slices ginger, shredded and finely chopped

3 cloves garlic, crushed and finely chopped

3 large spring onions (scallions), or baby leeks (see Our Secrets), slit lengthways then chopped into 2 cm/1 in pieces

½ tbsp sesame oil

½ tbsp stock

Our Secrets

On our first visit to Beijing, Auntie Meng-ch'i welcomed us with Mongolian Hot Pot, another dish that requires wafer-thin slices of lamb. To get the lamb wafer-thin, cut it into a slab, freeze until just firm, then slice it very finely.

In Northern China, spring onions are more like our baby leeks. Using leeks adds a fullness of flavour to the dish, but they should be cooked a little longer. Remove the lamb from the pan after searing, then cook the leeks separately with a little more sauce. Then return the lamb to the pan for a final toss.

Tiger Prawns with Asparagus

Serves 4

12 tiger prawns, shelled and deveined

pinch of salt

1 tsp *Shaoxing* (rice) wine or medium sherry

2 tsp cornflour (cornstarch)

2 tsp vegetable or peanut oil

vegetable oil for deep-frying

240 g/8 oz/1 cup asparagus, trimmed and cut on the diagonal into 2.5 cm/1 in pieces

100 ml/3½ fl oz/scant ½ cup enhanced fish, chicken or vegetable stock (see page 145 or 146)

pinch of rock or granulated sugar

1 tbsp light soy sauce

2 tsp sesame oil

coriander (cilantro) leaves to garnish

When you stir fry asparagus, it turns a rich green. Together with the delicate pink of the prawns, this is a visual feast even before you get on to savour its succulence.

Marinate the prawns in a mixture of the salt, wine, cornflour and 2 teaspoons of oil. Leave in the refrigerator for 30 minutes.

Heat the wok, then pour in the oil for deep-frying and heat gently. When the oil is just hot, throw in the prawns and cook gently until they change colour. Scoop out and set aside.

Discard the oil, leaving about 2 tablespoons in the wok. Add the asparagus and toss in the oil until it changes colour. Add the stock and sugar.

Bring to the boil and simmer for 1 minute so the stock reduces. Return the prawns to the pan with the soy sauce and sesame oil. Turn together for a further 30 seconds. Garnish with the chopped coriander (cilantro) leaves.

Our Secret

Young asparagus barely needs cooking. If it is older, cut the ends on the diagonal, then turn the stems a quarter turn every time you make a cut. This makes irregular-shaped pieces and increases the cut surfaces exposed to the heat. Cut this way the vegetables cook faster and absorb more sauce.

Duck in Mustard and Soy Sauce

Cooking with mustard is very common in China, but a little-known Oriental trick in the West.

Remove the fat and skin from the duck and discard it. Cut the meat across the fillets into 5 mm/¼ in slices.

Heat the oil in a wok or frying pan. When hot, turn the ginger in the oil then add the duck meat and stir fry for 1 minute. Remove the meat with a slotted spoon and put to one side.

Stir fry the garlic and leeks for 1½ minutes. Add the salt, butter, soy sauce, sugar, mustard and stock to the pan. Stir together until it becomes creamy and is bubbling.

Return the duck meat to the pan. Stir into the sauce and let it all simmer gently until the duck meat is cooked through.

Serves 3 with rice and another dish, such as a stir fried vegetable

360 g/12 oz/1½ cups duck breast

4 tbsp vegetable oil

3 slices fresh root ginger, finely shredded

2 cloves garlic, crushed and finely chopped

3 young leeks, cut lengthways then on the diagonal into 1 cm/½ in sections

1½ tsp salt

30 g/1 oz/2 tbsp butter or lard

2 tsp light soy sauce

2 tsp rock or granulated sugar

2 tbsp mustard, preferably Dijon (if you use mustard powder, use 3 parts mustard to 4 parts water and leave for at least 30 minutes before using)

2 tbsp good-quality chicken stock (see page 145)

Our Secrets

Our first taste of yellow mustard powder in Chinese food was when our teacher Zhang took us out for a meal in a restaurant frequented by government officials behind the Boulevard of Eternal Peace in Beijing. For this dish we recommend a prepared Dijon mustard.

Butter is our preferred substitute for the traditional lard. If you are not cholesterol conscious, render the duck fat by removing the oil glands from just inside the main cavity. Boil in a pan of water until the water boils dry, then strain the oil. Rendered fat gives a fuller, glossier taste and a fantastic flavour to roasted vegetables, particularly potatoes.

Yellow Cassia Roll

Serves 3

120 g/4 oz/½ cup lean
pork, cut into matchstick-
size shreds

2½ tbsp light soy sauce

pinch of salt and pepper

4 medium dried Chinese
mushrooms, soaked in hot
water for 30 minutes

4 tbsp vegetable
or peanut oil

60 g/2 oz wood ears,
soaked in hot water for
30 minutes

1 spring onion (scallion),
cut into 3 cm/1½ in
sections

50 g/2 oz golden needles

2 cloves garlic, crushed
and finely chopped

3 slices fresh root ginger,
finely chopped

½ tsp rock or granulated
sugar

2½ tbsp enhanced stock
(see page 147)

3 eggs, lightly beaten

1 tbsp *Shaoxing* (rice) wine
or medium sherry

1 tsp sesame oil

steamed pancakes (see
page 113)

2 tbsp sweet yellow bean
sauce to serve

One of our family favourites, which can be eaten as it is or wrapped in the steamed pancakes that are also used for Crispy Duck or Crispy Lamb wrapped in Lettuce (see page 60). Yellow cassia blossoms are simulated with the scrambled egg, which gives a tapestry effect when contrasted with wood ears and Chinese mushrooms. The pancakes can easily be bought and reheated by steaming for a few minutes while you prepare this wonderful dish. Alternatively, make your own (see page 113).

Marinate the pork for 20 minutes in the soy sauce, salt, pepper and 2 teaspoons of water. Drain the mushrooms, then discard the stalks. Cut the caps into similar-size shreds as the pork.

Heat the wok, then add 2 tablespoons of oil, swirling it round until it begins to smoke. Stir fry the mushrooms and pork for 1½ minutes. Add the wood ears, spring onion, golden needles, garlic, ginger, sugar and stock. Toss together for a further 1 minute, then remove from the heat.

Heat the remaining oil in a small pan and pour in the eggs. Heat over a steady heat until they begin to puff up. Break the egg up into small pieces, then transfer to the wok. Add the wine and sesame oil and turn together briefly.

Spread the pancakes with a little sweet yellow bean sauce before filling with a little of the pork mixture, then rolling up. This dish is just as good served with rice.

Our Secret
Victoria Conran, our recipe tester, has created a vegetarian version with needle mushrooms, the long, thin, light brown variety. We call this dish Three Fungi Roll.

Stir Fried Chicken and Broccoli

This is a good recipe for children, who seem to choose broccoli over other green vegetables. It emphasises the slightly sweet flavour and crunchy texture of the broccoli, while making a good colour contrast with the white flesh of the chicken. With celery, the dish is more savoury than sweet.

Cut the chicken against the grain into thin slices about 5 cm/2 in long. Sprinkle with 1 tablespoon of Shaoxing wine.

Mix the egg white with the chicken, adding ½ tablespoon of oil. Chill for 30 minutes in the refrigerator. Mix the soy sauce, oyster sauce, stock, cornflour, the remaining Shaoxing wine and sugar together, then pour into a pan.

Break the broccoli into individual florets, halving the larger ones and removing any thick stems. (If using celery, slice into pieces 5 cm x 5 mm/2 in x ¼ in.) Place in boiling water, bring back to a rolling boil then drain. Set aside.

Heat the wok until it smokes, then add the remaining oil. When it is warm enough to gently brown a cube of bread, throw in the chicken, pushing the pieces apart. Turn down the heat a little and leave to cook for about 40 seconds. As soon as the chicken completely changes colour remove with a slotted spoon.

Scatter the garlic and ginger into the pan and turn quickly in the oil. Add the broccoli and repeat. Return the chicken to the pan, bring back to the boil, then turn down the heat, simmering for a further 1 minute. Finally, glaze with sesame oil before serving.

Serves 3 with rice and another stir fried dish

240 g/8 oz/1 cup chicken breast

2 tbsp Shaoxing (rice) wine or medium sherry

½ egg white, lightly beaten with a pinch of salt, but not frothy

4 tbsp vegetable or peanut oil

½ tbsp light soy sauce

½ tbsp oyster sauce

2 tbsp enhanced chicken stock (see page 145)

½ tbsp cornflour (cornstarch)

½ tsp rock or granulated sugar

240 g/8 oz/1 cup broccoli or celery

2 cloves garlic, crushed and finely chopped

3 slices fresh root ginger, finely chopped

2 tsp sesame oil

Our Secrets

Each of our chefs has had their own special way of marinating meat and seafood before stir frying. Marinating in egg white tenderises chicken, but don't add too much egg white or it will congeal in the final stir fry. There should be just enough to coat the meat.

So long as you adjust to individual cooking times, by chopping finely, blanching or pre-cooking, it is possible to stir fry any vegetable. Mangetout need only a quick turn in the oil; broccoli needs to be blanched briefly, while aubergine (eggplant) must be stir fried then left to simmer gently until is has absorbed the liquid from the sauce.

Sliced Beef with Leeks and Mangetout

Serves 2–3

For the marinade:

¾ tsp salt

2 tbsp *Shaoxing* (rice) wine
or medium sherry

1 tbsp vegetable or
peanut oil

½ tbsp cornflour
(cornstarch)

pinch of pepper

240 g/8 oz/1 cup lean
beef, thinly sliced

4 tbsp vegetable or peanut
oil

3 cloves garlic, thinly
sliced

2–3 young leeks or
4 spring onions (scallions),
sliced lengthways, then
into 1 cm/½ in sections

120 g/4 oz/½ cup
mangetout, trimmed

1 tsp sesame oil

*A quick and easy meal when served with rice or noodles. It is a
substantial dish, but the combination of the glazed colours and
contrasting textures gives a delicate touch.*

Combine the marinade ingredients, add 1 tablespoon of water, then
marinate the beef for 15 minutes.

Heat the wok, then add the oil, swirling it round the pan. Stir in the
beef and garlic. Toss and turn quickly over a medium heat until all the
meat has browned.

Add the leeks and mangetout to the pan. Stir quickly until the leeks
wilt. Add a little *Shaoxing* wine if the sauce is too thick. Drizzle over
the sesame oil and serve.

Our Secret

Marinating the beef tenderises it and brings out its natural flavour.
If the marinade is strong enough it is not necessary to add extra
sauces during the stir fry. A dusting of cornflour will help the sauce
coat the meat, but don't use too much or it will stick to the pan.

Stir Fried Eggs with Radishes

You have never tasted scrambled eggs this good! The radishes make this a splendid feast of colour.

Combine the eggs with the salt and sugar. Heat the oil in the wok and when it begins to smoke, pour in the egg. Stir fry until it begins to solidify.

Add the vinegar, oyster sauce, wine and ginger. Turn again in the wok for a few seconds. Garnish with radishes.

Serves 2

4 eggs, beaten

½ tsp salt

1 tsp rock or granulated sugar

4 tbsp vegetable or peanut oil

1 tbsp rice or white wine vinegar

1 tsp oyster sauce

1 tsp *Shaoxing* (rice) wine or medium sherry

2 cm/1 in piece fresh root ginger, finely chopped

finely sliced radishes to garnish

Our Secret
If you want to impress guests, the formal method of preparing this dish is to separate the eggs. While you cook the yolk as above, steam the white separately until solid. Cut it into strips and add to the dish before serving.

Chinese Leaves with Bean Curd

Serves 4 as a side dish

3 tbsp vegetable or peanut oil

4 slices peeled fresh root ginger

240 g/8 oz/1 cup Chinese cabbage, cut on the diagonal into 2.5 cm x 5 cm/1 in x 2 in pieces

1 cake firm bean curd, blanched in boiling water and simmered for 1 minute, then cut into 4 cm x 2.5 cm x 2 cm/ 1½ in x 1 in x ¾ in pieces

1 tsp salt

¼ tsp rock or granulated sugar

2 tbsp light soy sauce

1 tsp vegetarian stock powder (bouillon)

1 tbsp *Shaoxing* (rice) wine or medium sherry

4 tsp sesame oil

Chinese leaves and bean curd make a basic side dish to go with almost any of the other dishes and rice. In this recipe, the bean curd is boiled to make it more tender and fluffy. For a crisp version, you could also use deep-fried bean curd.

Heat the oil in the wok until it almost smokes. Throw in the ginger and swish it around. Add the Chinese cabbage and bean curd. Toss gently for about 30 seconds.

Add the salt, sugar and soy sauce, then stir quickly for a further 30 seconds. Turn the heat down and add the stock powder and *Shaoxing* wine, turning all together with the Chinese cabbage.

Cover and simmer until the cabbage begins to look translucent and is tender and slightly crunchy. Glaze with sesame oil to serve.

Our Secrets

Northern Chinese hold Chinese cabbage in the same affection as English people reserve for Brussels sprouts. It must be cooked to perfection, neither under- nor overdone as they very quickly lose their crisp centre. So, if your stir fry is in danger of wilting, reduce the liquids separately.

This dish is quite salty, so go easy on any extra seasoning.

Gongbao's Chilli Pork

This is one of the classic Gongbao dishes that is a favourite the world over. Its secret lies in the rich savoury/sweet sauce, combined with the nutty taste of sesame. You could swap the meat for chicken and the nuts for peanuts or cashews without disturbing the integrity of this dish. Gongbao was an officer in the Imperial court to Sichuan and, for his leaving party, instructed his chef to entertain his friends with a new dish, the first of many Gongbao specialities.

Dry-fry the pine nuts until golden brown, stirring constantly. Set aside.

Combine the marinade ingredients, then marinate the pork in the refrigerator for 30 minutes.

Heat the wok, then add the oil. Scatter in the pork, then turn in the oil over a medium heat for about 40 seconds. Remove with a slotted spoon and keep warm. Reduce the heat.

Add the chilli peppers, pressing them down in the oil until they change colour (beware of spitting!). Add the ginger and sliced courgettes and keep tossing and turning in the oil for a further 1 minute. Pour away any excess oil.

Add the dark soy sauce, wine, vinegar, sugar, stock and salt. Bring to a vigorous boil. Return the meat to the pan, and continue to boil for a further 2 minutes. Glaze with sesame oil and scatter the pine nuts over to serve.

Our Secrets
Many Chinese chefs deep-fry the nuts in gongbao dishes. Although this gives an even golden colour, we prefer to dry-fry as it is less oily.

The benefit of marinating in cornflour is that you have no trouble in thickening the sauce. Soy and oil, in contrast, hydrate and seal the meat. When you fry the pork don't let it sizzle or the meat will harden.

Serves 4 with 2–3 other dishes and rice

75 g/2½ oz pine nuts (pine kernels)

For the marinade:

1 tbsp light soy sauce

1 tbsp cornflour (cornstarch)

1 tbsp vegetable or peanut oil

240 g/8 oz/1 cup pork fillet, sliced thinly across the grain and cut into 5 cm/2 in pieces

3 tbsp vegetable or peanut oil

4 red chilli peppers, seeded or 2 tsp hot bean paste

3 slices fresh root ginger, finely chopped

240 g/8 oz/1 cup courgettes (zucchini), sliced into thin half-moon shapes

1 tbsp dark soy sauce

1 tbsp *Shaoxing* (rice) wine or medium sherry

1 tbsp red wine vinegar

2 tsp rock or granulated sugar

3 tbsp strong stock or tsp stock powder (bouillon) dissolved in 3 tbsp of hot water

¼ tsp salt

1 tsp sesame oil

Scrambled Eggs with Tomatoes

Serves 4

2 large spring onions (scallions), white part only, finely sliced

½ tsp salt

4 free-range eggs, beaten

3 tbsp vegetable or peanut oil

5 tomatoes, quartered and seeded

1 tsp rock or granulated sugar

Here's a wholesome recipe for children who like junk food – an alternative to eggs and baked beans. They are always attracted to the vibrant combination of yellow and red, garnished with spring onions.

Mix the spring onions and salt with the eggs. Heat 2 tablespoons of oil in a wok over a high heat. When it is just beginning to smoke, pour in the egg mixture. As it swells, stir quickly to prevent it from burning.

As soon as the egg turns a golden colour, scoop it from the pan with a slotted spoon, and set aside. Turn the heat down.

Heat the remaining oil in the wok. Add the tomatoes, sugar and 2 tablespoons of water, then simmer until the tomatoes are soft. Return the eggs to the wok, breaking them up with a fork, and mix with the tomato.

Our Secret

This is a traditional supper or lunch dish, available at street cafés all over China. A grown-up version of this dish is to replace the tomatoes with spinach: stir fry 500 g/1 lb young spinach with a little salt and garlic until it wilts, before returning the eggs to the wok. Serve with rice and another dish.

'Three Sea-flavours' in Wine Sauce

Here is one of our father's favourite seafood dishes. The bright colours of the pepper and prawns (shrimp) complement its tangy flavour. Serve with rice and a green vegetable.

Sprinkle the seafood with salt and pepper and 1 tablespoon of oil. Heat the wok and add 3 tablespoons of oil. When it just begins to smoke, add the seafood. Stir fry quickly over a high heat for 1¾ minutes. Remove with a slotted spoon and set aside.

Add the ginger, garlic, spring onions and pepper to the pan. Turn them together quickly over a high heat. Add the soy sauce, wine and cornflour. Stir them together.

When the mixture starts to boil, return the seafood to the pan and stir for 1½ minutes. Sprinkle with sesame oil and serve immediately.

Serves 4

120 g/4 oz/½ cup large prawns (shrimp), shelled and deveined

4–5 scallops

120 g/4 oz/½ cup squid (calamari), cut roughly into rectangles

pinch each of salt and pepper

4 tbsp vegetable or peanut oil

2 slices fresh root ginger, finely chopped

2 cloves garlic, coarsely chopped

2 spring onions (scallions), cut into 2.5 cm/1 in sections

½ medium red (bell) pepper, cut into 2.5 cm x 2.5 cm/1 in x 1 in pieces

1 tbsp light soy sauce

3 tbsp dry white wine

½ tsp cornflour (cornstarch) blended with 3 tbsp water

1½ tsp sesame oil

Our Secret
If you cut the squid pieces with a criss-cross pattern, when cooked they will curl up into small cylinders. Father always delighted in the appearance of these seafood dishes: the vibrant tapestry of pinks, yellow, green, red and white emphasises the different textures. Wood ear (black fungus) is a delicious addition – its black floral curves contrast with the delicate shapes and colours of the seafood.

Mala Bean Curd

Serves 2 with other dishes

1 tbsp vegetable or
peanut oil

1 tsp hot bean paste or
chilli sauce

240 g/8 oz/1 cup silken
bean curd

2 large spring onions
(scallions), cut into
½ cm/¼ in pieces

2 tbsp dark soy sauce

½ tbsp light soy sauce

pinch of ground Sichuan
peppercorn

*This is a hot strong dish that should be served with plain rice or any
other plain staple. You should combine it with one or two other dishes.*

Heat the wok. Add the oil, then the hot bean paste. When it begins to
smoke, add the bean curd, gently breaking it up into chunks. Turn for
1 minute over a high heat.

Turn down the heat, then add the spring onions and soy sauces and
simmer for 2 minutes. Turn it out on to a dish and sprinkle with
Sichuan pepper. Stir before serving.

Our Secret
Mala is one of the characteristics of Sichuan cuisine, and refers to
the numbing heat of Sichuan pepper (*ma*) in combination with the
spiky heat of chilli (*la*). Of course, you can vary the Sichuan pepper,
chilli and soy sauce to taste. Sichuan pepper must be dry-roasted
before crushing with a mortar and pestle. Stored in a sealed jar, it will
retain its flavour for several months.

Gongbao Diced Chicken with Walnuts

This is a fail-safe dish for any occasion. It looks gorgeous with the shining yellows and reds contrasting with the glistening white chicken, and it tastes great. The crunchy nuts beautifully complement the sweet, plump peppers.

Combine the egg white, salt and 1 tablespoon of soy sauce, then stir in the chicken. Marinate in the refrigerator for 30 minutes. Combine the vinegar, wine, sugar, remaining soy sauce and cornflour.

Heat the wok. Add just enough oil to grease the pan. Add the walnuts and stir fry gently for about 1 minute. Remove and drain on kitchen paper (kitchen towels). If there is any residue from the nuts, wipe the wok.

Pour the remaining oil into the wok and heat through. Add the chicken, pushing the pieces gently apart. Stir fry over a medium heat for about 2½ minutes or until all the chicken is browned. Remove with a slotted spoon and set aside in a warm place. Pour away any excess oil.

Toss the ginger, spring onions and peppers into the pan and stir together for 30 seconds. Add the wine and vinegar mixture and give it all a good toss. Return the chicken to the pan and stir with the other ingredients for 2 minutes over a high heat. Finally, scatter over the walnuts.

Serves 3 with one other dish and rice

½ egg white

½ tsp salt

3 tbsp dark soy sauce

500 g/1 lb/3 cups chicken breast, cut into walnut-size chunks

2 tsp red wine vinegar

4 tbsp *Shaoxing* (rice) wine or medium sherry

2 tsp rock or granulated sugar

1 tbsp cornflour (cornstarch)

5 tbsp vegetable or peanut oil

180 g/6 oz/1½ cups whole or halved walnuts

2–3 slices fresh root ginger, shredded

3 spring onions (scallions), cut lengthways then into 4 cm/1½ in sections

1 small yellow (bell) pepper, cut into walnut-size squares

1 small red (bell) pepper, cut into walnut-size squares

Our Secrets

A competent stir fry chef keeps a number of small bowls of favourite ingredients by the cooker and can distinguish between salt and sugar at a glance. If you are stir frying a number of dishes, it is easy to become confused as to the different ingredients. The best way is to have a number of platters of varying sizes from very small for ginger and garlic through to dishes big enough to take all the vegetables. You can also pre-mix sauces.

Make sure the walnuts are whole or halved; if they are cut into smaller pieces they will burn during the stir frying process.

Casseroles and Oven Cooking

Food to come home to

Casseroling is a term that evokes the iron ranges of rural kitchens in the South of France and Northern Italy and the smell of rabbit and red wine. It is all these associations of country and home-cooking that we hope to draw on in calling this section Casserole and Oven Cooking. For *geng* (meat stew), cooked in traditional sandpots, is one of the most time-honoured techniques in Chinese cuisine. Oriental aromas are more complex, but there are obvious similarities between those European cuisines and the Chinese tradition of long-cooking and red-braising: meats are simmered slowly over a hob or gently stewed or roasted in the oven until the flesh is so tender that it falls away from the bone and melts in your mouth. And the seasonings and long-cooking of the bones gives the sauce a richness that cannot be simulated in any other way.

For clarity we define casseroling as any dish that takes longer than, say, ten minutes and requires covering with a lid. A casserole, therefore, may simply be an extended stir fry or a slow cooked dish, started over a high heat on the hob, then seasoned and transferred to the oven for a long, slow stew. It takes at least a couple of hours to nurture and mature this kind of casserole, but these are great dishes worth every minute of the preparation time.

Traditionally the Chinese did not have ovens and meats such as roast pork, duck or suckling pig were roasted comercially or in the restaurant kitchens. The key to the special quality of Chinese roast meats is to marinade them first in a mixture of spices and soy products such as soy sauce, hoisin or fermented bean curd.

Where Chinese casseroling is distinctive is in the layers of subtle and not so subtle flavouring. Long-cooked meats are naturally sweet and only need a touch of sugar to bring out their fragrance. The danger is always in being too heavy-handed with the salt, dark soy and ginger and reducing everything to a one dimensional stew. With less soy the unique flavours of the dried ingredients can seep through the whole dish. Red dates, the most commonly grown fruit in stone age China, give a deep-muffled sweetness; tangerine peel offers its sharper, rounder, tangy richness; dried mushrooms, provide a unique, slightly musty savouriness and the after-taste of aniseed cleans and lightens up the palate even when the dish is long gone. Many of these are the herbs and fruits that were already available in the kitchens of early imperial China, two thousand years ago. But perhaps the most healing effect of a good casserole is the aroma that welcomes you home after a long hard day's work in the winter.

Knuckle of Pork with Red Dates and Bak Choy

This is our version of an award-winning dish that father and his first chef created. The addition of red dates brings a delicate fruity sweetness to the rich savoury pork. Serve this with plain boiled rice as the central spread for a hearty meal for those who are not afraid of rich meats.

Preheat the oven to 170°C/325°F/Gas 3. Clean the pork and put it in a pan of boiling water. Return to the boil, then simmer for 20 minutes. Drain and rub the pork with 2 tablespoons of soy sauce. Put to one side for 30 minutes.

Heat the oil in a heavy frying pan (skillet) and slowly fry the knuckle for 8–10 minutes until it is quite brown on all sides.

Heat the stock in a deep casserole. When hot, add the pork and red dates, together with the ginger, onion, star anise, sugar, remaining soy sauce and salt. Cover and cook gently in the oven for 2 hours, turning the meat every 30–45 minutes.

Remove the pork and place it in the centre of a serving dish. Transfer the casserole to the hob (stove). Add the wine to the meat juices and reduce the sauce over a high heat until it is thick and glistening.

Meanwhile, stir fry the bak choy. Heat the oil in the wok, swirling it around until it starts to smoke. Add the garlic and turn in the oil, then add the white part of the bak choy. Stir fry for 30 seconds, then turn down the heat. Add the remaining green part of the vegetables with the stock and sugar and turn up the heat as high as possible, turning together for a further minute. Arrange the bak choy around the edge of the serving dish.

Pour the sauce over the pork and serve.

Our Secret

Ideally, the pork should be brought to the table glazed with a thick and glistening sauce. It is difficult to prescribe the amount of fluids that you need for a sauce. Many factors intervene: the amount of fluid in different cuts of meat or vegetable varies enormously; some soy sauces are thicker than others and ovens are notoriously inaccurate and you must adjust the cooking time to the foibles of your own. Using the technique of reducing allows you to control the consistency exactly. You can also adjust the seasoning at this point. With this recipe it is the rock sugar that enhances the glazed finish.

Serves 5–6

1 x 1.8 kg/4 lb knuckle of pork, cut well up into the leg

5½ tbsp dark soy sauce

1 tbsp vegetable or peanut oil

750 ml/1¼ pints/3 cups enhanced chicken stock (see page 145)

20 red dates

2–3 slices fresh root ginger, chopped

1 large onion, sliced

3–4 heads star anise

1 tbsp rock or granulated sugar

1 tsp salt

2–3 tbsp *Shaoxing* (rice) wine or medium sherry

For the bed of greens:

3 tbsp vegetable or peanut oil

2 cloves garlic, crushed and finely chopped

250 g/9 oz/1 cup bak choy, washed, dried and leaves separated from the stalks

1 tbsp good-quality stock

½ tsp rock or granulated sugar

Angelica Lamb Stew

casseroles and oven cooking

Serves 4–6

20 g/¾ oz Chinese
angelica (*dang gui*),
soaked in cold water
for 30 minutes

5 Chinese dried
mushrooms, soaked in hot
water for 30 minutes

400 g/14 oz shoulder or
leg of lamb (off the bone),
cut into 3 cm/1¼ in cubes

1½ tbsp vegetable or
peanut oil

2 cm/¾ in cube fresh root
ginger, finely sliced

1 large piece tangerine
peel, soaked in hot water
for 30 minutes

300 ml/10 fl oz/1¼ cups
lamb or chicken stock

1½ tbsp dark soy sauce

pinch of sugar

½ tbsp yellow bean paste

2 tbsp *Shaoxing* (rice) wine
or medium sherry

90 g/3 oz cooked
chestnuts

Chinese angelica or dang gui *is beginning to make an impact on the Western health food and medicine market. This recipes represents the great tradition of cooking with medicinal herbs and the intimate relationship between food and medicine in Chinese culture. Tangerine peel is also warming and a good expectorant. This dish is not only a substantial and tasty lamb stew, but it will also restore your energy and resources.*

Drain and squeeze the angelica. Wrap in muslin (cheesecloth) and secure with thin string. Discard the hard mushroom stalks and halve the caps. Cook the lamb in boiling water for 3 minutes, then drain.

Heat the oil in a casserole. When it begins to smoke, scatter in the ginger and turn in the oil. Add the lamb and turn together for a further 3–4 minutes.

Add the tangerine peel, Chinese mushrooms, stock, soy sauce, sugar, yellow bean paste, wine, Chinese angelica and chestnuts. Bring to the boil and simmer gently for 2 hours, stirring occasionally.

Our Secret
There is a good dose of *dang gui* in this stew. If you don't like the taste, but feel you need the remedy, boil it for 30 minutes after soaking, then add the strained liquid in small amounts to any soup or stew.

Lobster with Ginger and Shanghai Noodles (page 92)

White Fungus and Cucumber Salad (page 81) and

Knuckle of Pork with Red Dates and Bak Choy (page 31)

Black Bean Seafood (page 95) and Chilli French Beans (page 70)

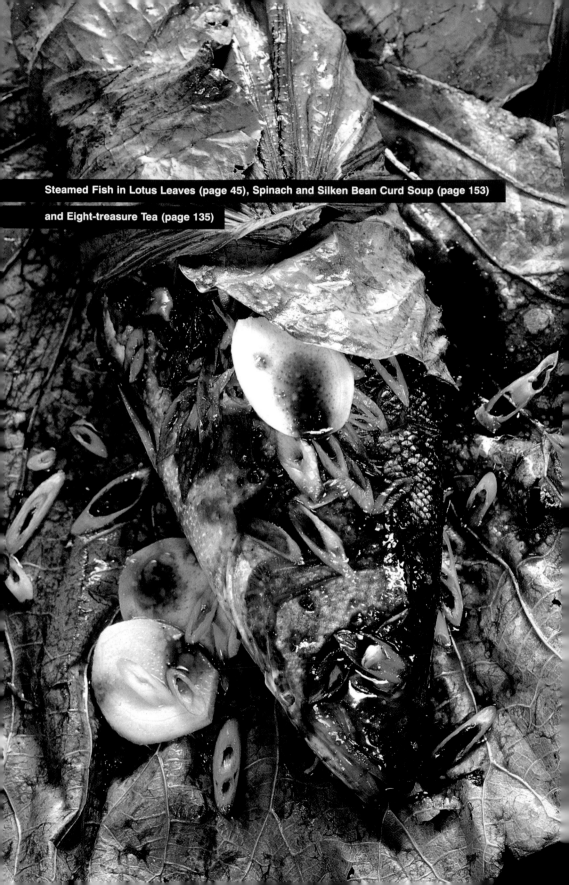

Steamed Fish in Lotus Leaves (page 45), Spinach and Silken Bean Curd Soup (page 153) and Eight-treasure Tea (page 135)

Chicken Chilli Mountain (page 59)

Tangerine Duck

This is classic homely fare, simple to prepare but rich and satisfying. The skin of the duck is rubbed with soy and oil, then roasted to colour deeply. Rock sugar then gives a final glaze. You can substitute the peel and celery with dried mushrooms. For a sweeter version use pre-soaked and boiled chestnuts (see page 9), or fresh pineapple. Use the duck fat for roasting potatoes.

Preheat the oven to 200°C/400°F/Gas 6. Remove the duck's tail and the oil glands from just inside its back opening. Trim the neck skin. Dry the duck inside and out with kitchen paper (kitchen towels), then rub with 1–2 tablespoons of the dark soy sauce and all of the oil, so that it is dark and glistening.

Place the onions into the cavity of the duck. Place the duck directly on the middle shelf of the oven with a pan underneath to catch the fat. Roast for 25 minutes.

Drain the tangerine or pomelo peel and make a bed of peel and celery for the duck in the bottom of a deep casserole. Add the water or stock, remaining soy sauces, *Shaoxing* wine, orange juice, star anise and ginger. Season with salt and add the oyster sauce, if using. Bring to the boil.

Add the duck, breast down, then turn the heat down to a slow simmer for 1 hour. Add the rock sugar and turn the duck over, spooning off any fat from the surface. Cook for a further hour.

When the duck is nearly cooked, quickly stir fry the Chinese cabbage and arrange on either end of a large serving dish.

Remove the duck and joint it. Carefully remove the breast, leaving the delicate skin intact. Arrange the duck on the plate and cut it into bite-sized pieces. Reduce the sauce by boiling vigorously, then remove the peel. When it is thick and glossy, strain it over the duck.

Our Secret

Dried tangerine or pomelo peel imparts a fuller, deeper flavour than lemon peel. It is also less tart. It isn't good to eat the peel itself, so you can remove it before serving. It is satisfying to sun-dry your own peel, but make sure you leave them until really hard and dry. (You can speed up the process in a hot oven.)

Serves 4

1 x 1.8 kg/4 lb duck

4 tbsp dark soy sauce

2 tbsp light soy sauce

1½ tbsp vegetable or peanut oil

2 Spanish onions, thickly sliced

4 large pieces dried tangerine or pomelo peel, soaked in hot water for 30 minutes

2 celery sticks, washed and thickly sliced on the diagonal

250 ml/8 fl oz/1 cup water, chicken or duck stock

600 ml/1 pint/2½ cups *Shaoxing* (rice) wine or medium sherry

juice of 2 oranges

3 whole star anise

4 cm/1½ in piece fresh root ginger, thickly sliced

1 tsp salt

1½ tbsp oyster sauce (optional)

4 tbsp rock sugar or granulated sugar

Chinese cabbage to garnish

Soy-braised Beef Stew

Serves 4

5 large Chinese dried mushrooms

1½ tbsp vegetable or peanut oil

500 g/1 lb stewing beef, cut into 5 cm x 2.5 cm/2 in x 1 in chunks

240 g/8 oz/1 cup carrots, thickly sliced

1 tbsp dark soy sauce

2 tsp hoisin sauce

½ tbsp rock sugar or granulated sugar

2 tbsp *Shaoxing* (rice) wine or medium sherry

2 heads star anise

300 ml/10 fl oz/1¼ cups beef or chicken stock

2 tsp yellow bean sauce

6 pieces previously deep-fried and dried firm bean curd (optional)

2 spring onions (scallions), finely chopped

Here is a beef stew with plenty of stamina and lots of different textures. Serve it on a winter's day with rice or mantou (see page 49) and a stir-fried vegetable.

Preheat the oven to 200ºC/400ºF/Gas 6. Soak the mushrooms in hot water for 30 minutes, then remove any hard stalks and quarter the caps. Reserve the soaking liquid.

Heat the oil in a large casserole. When hot, add the beef and carrots. Stir them over a high heat for a couple of minutes. Add the soy sauce, hoisin sauce, sugar, wine, star anise, mushrooms and their soaking water, stock and yellow bean sauce. Mix with the beef and carrots. Bring to the boil and then remove the casserole from the hob (stove) and put into the oven.

Cook for 30 minutes, then reduce the heat to 170ºC/325ºF/Gas 3. Cook, covered, for a further 2 hours, stirring once or twice.

If you are using the bean curd, strain the sauce from the meat. Place the meat on a preheated serving dish and heat the sauce in a pan with the bean curd. Reduce the liquid until thick and shiny then pour back, with the bean curd, over the meat. Scatter with the chopped spring onions to serve.

Our Secret

Light soy sauce is stronger-tasting than the dark and a little is added to light-coloured sauces with vegetables, chicken or fish. Here dark soy sauce is used to give the beef stew a good strong colour. When mixed with hoisin sauce the effect is to add a sweet piquancy rather than to increase the saltiness. It also gives a reddish brown hue and a creamy consistency.

Chicken and Chestnut Casserole

A lovely winter dish, this is simple to prepare and takes less than an hour to cook. You only have to remember to soak the chestnuts in advance. These give a gorgeous, mildly sweet flavour made exotic by the addition of a little star anise.

Pour plenty of boiling water over the chestnuts and soak them overnight. Bring them to the boil in fresh water and simmer for 1 hour before using. Soak the mushrooms in hot water for 30 minutes, remove any hard stalks, quarter the caps and reserve the soaking liquid.

Cut through the skin and flesh of the chicken where the wings and legs joins the main body, then snap back the joint and cut between the heads of the bones.

Turn the body on to its side and, using a heavy chopping knife or cleaver, divide it lengthways through the middle where the breast meets the back. Divide the breasts by cutting along the central line lengthways and peeling back the flesh. Pull away all the skin.

Heat the oil in a large casserole. Toss the ginger and onions in the oil. Add the chicken pieces and turn in the oil until all the surfaces have changed colour.

Add the sugar, salt, soy sauce, star anise, wine and 250 ml/8 fl oz/ 1 cup hot water, then mix to cover the chicken. Add the chestnuts and mushrooms, plus soaking water. Bring to the boil, cover and simmer for 40 minutes, stirring gently from time to time. (If the sauce is too liquid, strain it and reduce to thicken.)

Serve with rice and a light green vegetable.

Serves 4

180 g/6 oz/¾ cup dried unsalted chestnuts or 360 g/12 oz fresh chestnuts

60 g/2 oz Chinese dried mushrooms

1 medium chicken, or the equivalent weight in chicken thighs

3 tbsp vegetable or peanut oil

4 slices fresh root ginger

1 medium onion, sliced

1 tbsp rock or granulated sugar

pinch of salt

5 tbsp dark soy sauce

1 head star anise

100 ml/3½ fl oz/scant ½ cup *Shaoxing* (rice) wine or medium sherry

Our Secret
For these kind of casseroles, free-range chickens are immeasurably better. Our mother raises chickens herself and even her toughest old cocks are a delicacy when cooked in this way in her Rayburn. You simply have to increase the cooking time so that the dark flesh softens gently.

Lamb in Cumin Sesame Cream Sauce

Serves 3–4 with rice and a vegetable dish

4 cloves garlic, crushed and finely chopped

6 slices fresh root ginger, finely chopped

2 tbsp sesame paste, or dark tahini (see Our Secrets)

300 ml/10 fl oz/1¼ cups cold enhanced lamb or chicken stock (see page 145)

3 tbsp peanut oil

500 g/1 lb cubed, boned stewing lamb (shoulder or leg)

½ medium Spanish onion, peeled and finely chopped

2 tsp hot bean paste or chilli sauce

1½ tsp ground cumin

1½ tbsp light soy sauce

1½ tsp soft brown sugar

handful of fresh coriander (cilantro) leaves to garnish

This is our recreation of a spicy dish we enjoyed one New Year in a famous Moslem restaurant in Tianjin. There must be a Middle Eastern influence as it is reminiscent of a very similar old Persian curry made with almonds and cream. We felt it should be served with yoghurt and rice although that was not the way it was presented to us.

Blend or beat together the garlic, ginger, sesame paste, soy sauce and stock until smooth.

Heat the oil in a casserole and fry the meat until it changes colour on all sides. Remove with a slotted spoon and set aside.

Fry the onion until it turns brown. Add the blended liquid paste, hot bean paste, cumin, soy sauce and sugar. When it begins to bubble, return the meat to the pan. Bring back to the boil and reduce to a very slow simmer. Simmer for at least 1½ hours until the meat is very tender. Scatter with coriander (cilantro) to serve. (You can also cook this in the oven preheated to 180°C/350°F/Gas 4 for the same amount of time.)

Our Secrets

Granny He would spend all day cooking for three generations of her family who lived in two rooms next door to us in Beijing. Wafts of fragrant sesame, lamb, cumin and coriander (cilantro) greeted you whenever you passed her front door.

If you don't have any sesame paste you can use dark tahini although the latter combination is rather more reminiscent of West African cuisine, especially when served with chilli.

Honey Roast Pork

This is our version of Cha shao *pork, the little bits of red-edged meat that turn up in almost every takeaway dish. Normally, restaurants use red colouring agents sold in Chinese supermarkets in a set of silver coloured jars worthy of the chemistry lab. Here we just use honey, yellow bean and hoisin sauces which only muster a deep brownish tinge, less dramatic than red, but subtle and scrumptious.*

Place the pork in a shallow dish. Mix all the ingredients for the marinade in a bowl and then rub all over the meat. Leave to marinate for at least 2 hours, preferably overnight.

Preheat the oven to 220°C/425°F/Gas 7. Place the pork on a wire rack over a roasting tin filled with 2.5 cm/1 in water to catch the drips, and roast for 15 minutes. Turn the meat over, reduce the heat to 180°C/350°F/Gas 4 and roast for a further 30 minutes. Remove the pork and cut across the grain into thin slices. The meat should be edged with dark brown, contrasting appealingly with the lightly roasted colour of the inside.

Serves 4

500 g/1 lb pork fillet, cut into 2 pieces about 18 cm x 6 cm (7 in x 2½ in)

For the marinade:

2 cloves garlic, crushed and finely chopped

1 cm/½ in piece fresh root ginger, finely chopped

1 tbsp dark soy sauce

1 tbsp yellow bean paste

2 tbsp hoisin sauce

1 tbsp rock or granulated sugar

1½ tbsp vegetable or peanut oil

1 tsp red fermented bean curd

2 tbsp clear honey

1 tsp five-spice powder

Our Secret
Dad always kept a plate of cold meats hidden in the kitchen, ready to serve plain, stir fried or in soup. Since there is no need to serve the pork warm, leave it to cool before you slice it. As it cools the flesh firms and it is much easier to manage. If you cut it hot you also lose a lot of moisture in evaporation and run the risk of drying the meat. If you know you are not going to use it immediately, wrap in foil and slice just before serving.

Monkfish Casserole

Serves 4

3 tbsp vegetable or peanut oil

1 kg/2¼ lb monkfish, cut into 4 steaks

4 large spring onions (scallions), sliced lengthways and roughly chopped

6 slices fresh root ginger, shredded

4 cloves garlic, crushed and roughly chopped

1 tsp Sichuan peppercorns, roasted and ground (see page 10)

6 Chinese dried mushrooms, soaked for 30 minutes in water, stalks removed and caps halved

1 piece tangerine or pomelo peel

6 tbsp dark soy sauce

1 tbsp *Shaoxing* (rice) wine or medium sherry

4 tbsp *Zhengjiang*, balsamic or red wine vinegar

1 tbsp rock or granulated sugar

1 tsp salt

250 ml/8 fl oz/1 cup fish or chicken stock

120 g/4 oz/½ cup silken bean curd, cubed

sesame oil to glaze

coriander (cilantro) to garnish

This is an elegant casserole, simple to prepare, robust and flavoursome. You can use any soft, white fish and even whole sea bass cut into steaks. Obviously you have to vary the cooking time to the cut and quality of the fish. Monkfish is ideal as the outside turns brown while inside the flesh remains oily white just like the bean curd. Both look brilliant against the fresh green of the coriander (cilantro).

Heat the oil in the wok or a heavy casserole until it smokes. Carefully add the fish steaks and fry for 1 minute on each side.

Scatter in the spring onions, ginger, garlic, peppercorns, mushrooms and tangerine peel. Turn gently with the fish. Pour in the soy sauce, *Shaoxing* wine, vinegar, sugar, salt and stock and bring to the boil. Cover and simmer gently for 10 minutes.

Add the bean curd and baste with the liquid. Bring back to the boil and then turn off the heat. Cover and leave to stand for 5 minutes.

Glaze with the sesame oil and garnish with a small handful of coriander (cilantro).

Our Secret
The fish will be swimming in a rich broth which is perfect to serve with rice. For a thicker, glossy broth, along with the bean curd, add 1 tbsp cornflour (cornstarch) dissolved in cold water or, preferably, rice flour dissolved in cold water and then mixed with a little of the broth before adding to the casserole. In general, we prefer to reduce sauces rather than to copy the majority of restaurants chefs who almost always add cornflour to a casserole or stir fry. Our way is time consuming but tastier.

Red-braised Pork with Chestnuts

In our childhood, there was nothing so warming as to come home on a cold winter's day to a big bowl of rice and long-cooked belly pork. In ancient China fatty meat was a sign of wealth as it indicated that the household had enough money to feed the livestock well! The fat of this belly of pork becomes steeped in the juices of the meat and the sweet and savoury flavour of chestnut and soy, producing a rich succulent dish.

Pour plenty of boiling water over the chestnuts and leave them to soak overnight.

Bring the chestnuts to the boil in fresh water and simmer for 1 hour before using.

Clean the pork and slice it into strips about 2 cm/¾ in wide.

Fry the pork very gently in its own fat in a flameproof casserole until it browns a little on each side to seal the meat. Add 1 litre/1¾ pints/ 4 cups water, bring to the boil and simmer for 20 minutes. Discard the water.

Add the remaining ingredients and bring back to the boil. Put the casserole in the oven preheated to 170°C/325°F/Gas 3 and cook gently for at least 1½ hours.

Serves 4

20 Chinese dried chestnuts (or use fresh or canned and add towards the end of cooking)

500 g/1 lb belly of pork

1 tbsp dark soy sauce

1 tbsp whole five-spice

750 ml/1¼ pints/3 cups chicken stock

1½ tsp rock or granulated sugar

1 tbsp *Shaoxing* (rice) wine or medium sherry

Our Secret
The dark fragrance of five-spice and meats gently simmering until the flesh falls away from the bone will always conjure up images of father's smiling face at the door of the kitchen, cradling a casserole as if it were his special offering to the gods. With fatty meat the longer you leave the casserole to cook the more tender the meat. Check every now and then and add a little water if the liquid has reduced too much. If the sauce is very runny pour it off and reduce over a high heat, then return to the casserole. The meat should be very tender while the chestnuts should be soft but still firm.

Mapo Bean Curd

Serves 4

2 tbsp vegetable or
peanut oil

120 g/4 oz/½ cup minced
pork

2 slices fresh root ginger,
finely chopped

2 cloves garlic, crushed
and finely chopped

2 tsp hot bean paste or
chilli sauce

1 tbsp *Shaoxing* (rice) wine
or medium sherry

2 tbsp light soy sauce

400 g/14 oz firm bean
curd, cut into 2 cm/¾ in
cubes, soaked in boiling
water for 20 minutes and
drained

pinch of ground
Sichuan pepper

½ spring onion (scallion),
finely sliced

½ tsp sesame oil

*This dish was invented in the last century by the Chen family, who still
have a restaurant in Chengdu. The original Sichuanese version is
generally too hot for the Western palate, but here is our slightly tamer
but none the less delectable version.*

Heat the wok or casserole and add the oil. When it just begins to
smoke, add the pork and stir until it changes colour.

Add the ginger, garlic and hot bean paste and stir fry for about
4 minutes. Pour in 150 ml/5fl oz/⅔ cup water, the wine and soy
sauce. Bring to the boil and simmer for 4 minutes.

Add the bean curd to the wok and toss gently. Bring to the boil again
and simmer for a further 5 minutes. Season with pepper, scatter the
spring onion over and sprinkle with sesame oil to serve.

Our Secret
Bean curd always needs to be prepared before the final stir fry,
unless it is the soft Japanese versions that come in cartons.
Deep-frying makes it crisp and golden brown – moreish just by itself.
Blanching, as in this recipe, softens and hydrates it.

For a spicy vegetarian version you can use *zha cai*, the hot Sichuan
pickle. But wash it well to remove some of the powdered chilli.

Soya Pork

Here is another very common dish for which every family has a recipe. In this version, the sauce is cooked to perfection. And every minute of the steaming is worthwhile.

Wipe the pork, then soak it in cold water for 30 minutes. Rinse, then place in a large pan of water. Bring to the boil, then simmer gently for 20 minutes. Strain.

Add another 750 ml/1¼ pints/3 cups water and the remaining ingredients. Bring to the boil. Turn down the heat and simmer gently for 1½ hours, turning and basting the meat from time to time. The juices should become thick and syrupy. Add more water if necessary.

Transfer the meat and juices to a heatproof dish and place in a steamer. Steam for 30 minutes. Cut the meat finely. Remove the cinnamon stick and spring onion and serve with the sauce drizzled over the chopped meat or separately in a sauceboat (gravy boat).

Serves 4

750 g/1½ lb boned leg of pork

3 tbsp dark soy sauce

½ tbsp *Zhengjiang*, red or balsamic vinegar (see Our Secret)

1 tsp salt

pinch of Sichuan peppercorns, dry roasted and crushed (see page 10)

2 heads star anise

1 small cinnamon stick

1 spring onion (scallion)

2 tsp ground ginger

100 g/3½ oz/½ cup rock sugar or granulated sugar

Our Secret
Zhenjiang vinegar is really incomparable, but many English people find the odour overpowering. It is the best choice for dipping dumplings and plain cooked meats. An acceptable substitute is red wine vinegar, but balsamic vinegar has an equivalent distinctive mellow flavour.

Steaming

Cooking with delicacy

Steaming offers us the most romantic images of Chinese food; on a winter morning, the sight of billowing steam at the roadside will draw a crowd in the hope of a breakfast of pork and prawn (shrimp) dumplings with vinaigrette dips. And in Southern China families and friends often lunch around stacked bamboo steamers of assorted size, chopsticks at the ready.

In overseas Chinatowns, where most of the immigrant population come from the southern provinces, dimsum, the collection of steamed and deep fried snacks, are on the menu from mid morning right through the afternoon. There might be spring rolls, translucent steamed shrimp (prawn) dumplings, steamed pork wrapped in yellowy dough skins or fluffy white wheat buns stuffed with sweet roasted meats.

But while good dimsum are among the most complicated of Chinese recipes, there are plenty of steamed dishes that are authentic, scrumptious and easy to prepare. We would like to introduce steaming at its most simple and useful; you can, for example, re-hydrate and heat yesterday's meats or plain boiled rice with steam without damage to the original lightness and consistency of the dish. It is the plainest and most simple of cooking techniques.

Whatever type of steamer you use – a heatproof bowl on a stand inside a covered wok; a stack of baskets in your wok (or a selection of the smaller ones which will fit over the top of a saucepan) or aluminium (aluminum) or steel steamers designed to fit inside standard saucepans – the main thing is to start steaming with vigorously boiling water and to keep it at least 2.5 cm/1 in below the bottom of the steamer. In a long steam make sure the water does not boil dry. Do not add cold water to the boiling water in a steamer as this will reduce the temperature and prolong the cooking time.

Steamed Fish in Lotus Leaves

Here is a fantastic recipe for those times when you really want to impress! You can use any white fish – sea bass or a fat trout would be best – but it must be fresh off the rod. It looks good as the centrepiece of a number of dishes, served with rice.

Mix the salt, soy sauce, hoisin sauce, oil and wine together. Rub the fish inside and out with the mixture and leave to marinate for 30 minutes. Cover the fish with the spring onions and the slices of ginger.

Stir fry the onion, bacon and mushrooms in the butter for 1½ minutes, then stuff this mixture into the cavity of the fish.

Wrap the fish in the lotus leaves and secure with the string. Place in a heatproof dish in a steamer and steam for 25 minutes. When it is ready, cut open the string and leaves and baste with any liquid that has collected in the dish.

Bring to the table in the bamboo steamer or on a plate still wrapped in the lotus leaves.

Our Secrets

The length of steaming depends on the size of the fish. Calculate about 20 minutes per 500g/1lb for a light, fresh result.

Lotus leaves make an ideal wrapper, but you can use bamboo or any large culinary leaf such as lemon. Its intrinsic taste will delicately flavour the flesh of the fish. You can, of course, use foil. But you won't achieve those special flavours.

Serves 3

1 tsp salt

2 tbsp dark soy sauce

2 tbsp hoisin sauce

2 tbsp vegetable or peanut oil

2 tbsp *Shaoxing* (rice) wine or medium sherry

750 g/1½ lb whole sea bass, trout or grey mullet, cleaned and de-scaled

3 spring onions (scallions), shredded

8 slices fresh root ginger

For the stuffing:

1 onion, finely sliced

2 rashers bacon, or equivalent amount of preserved cabbage (snow pickle), finely sliced

120 g/4 oz/½ cup mushrooms, roughly chopped

1½ tbsp butter

2 lotus leaves, soaked in hot water for 10 minutes to soften, drained and dried

rough string

Lamb with Sichuan Peppercorns

Serves 4

500 g/1 lb lean loin of
lamb, preferably in one
piece, or 4 chops

2½ tbsp sesame oil

1 tsp whole Sichuan
peppercorns

½ onion

2 slices fresh root ginger

2 heads star anise

1½ tbsp *Shaoxing* (rice)
wine or medium sherry

2 tbsp light soy sauce

pinch of salt

150 ml/5 fl oz/⅔ cup lamb
stock

watercress for garnish

*Here, delicately flavoured lamb is both boiled and steamed in a gravy
flavoured with pepper and sesame oil until the meat is soft and
melting. Even though the dish has a European feel, as if it should be
served with potatoes, the flavour of Sichuan peppercorns is an
intoxicating reminder of the East.*

Bring a pan of water to the boil. Add the lamb, cover and simmer
gently for 45 minutes. Drain and keep the stock, reducing it by half.
Slice the meat into 5 mm/¼ in slices, but do not cut right through.
Place in a heatproof dish with the skin uppermost and set aside in a
warm place. (If you are using chops slice them in a similar way and
arrange in the dish).

To prepare the gravy, heat 1 tablespoon of sesame oil over a medium
heat. Throw in the Sichuan peppercorns and turn constantly for
30 seconds. Add the onion, ginger and star anise and turn them
around until you can smell the spicy aroma. Add the *Shaoxing* wine,
soy sauce, salt and lamb stock. Bring to the boil.

Pour the gravy over the lamb. Place the heatproof dish in a steamer
and steam vigorously for 20 minutes. Strain the liquid into a pan and
reduce it quickly over a high heat until thick and shiny. Pour the gravy
over the meat and glaze with the remaining sesame oil.

Garnish with watercress. Serve with rice and a vegetable.

Our Secrets
The taste for casseroled lamb comes from the influence of the
Northern and North-Western nomadic peoples. Wheat, which also
grows on the northern plains, is used in unleavened breads, such as
laobing (see page 112), which are often served with casseroles to
soak up the gravy.

Sichuan pepper is generally used to flavour the oil first. Only buy
seeded peppercorns, because the flavour comes from the husk.
Sometimes the whole husks are scattered into hot oil until they
change colour, then discarded.

Aubergine (Eggplant) with Bean Curd Sauce

Don't be put off by the sight and smell of fermented bean curd. When it is cooked it is not strong tasting and gives a delicious flourish to the plain steamed aubergine (eggplant).

Crush the bean curd and sprinkle with sugar, then mix with 2 tablespoons of water.

Place the aubergine (eggplant) chunks on a plate in a steamer and steam, for about 20 minutes, until soft.

When the aubergine (eggplant) is nearly done, heat the oil in a pan and add the bean curd sauce. Stir to mix and then add the aubergine, turning gently to coat with the sauce. Turn out on to a serving dish and sprinkle with coriander (cilantro).

Serves 4 as a side dish

3 pieces red or white fermented bean curd

1 tsp rock or granulated sugar

2 aubergines (eggplants), cut into 2 cm x 4 cm/¾ in x 1½ in chunks

1 tbsp vegetable or peanut oil

chopped coriander (cilantro), to garnish

Our Secrets

Fermented bean curd can be eaten straight from the jar with boiled rice, but this is not for the faint of heart. Just a little of the juice in the jar added to pork and vegetable stir fries gives an extra depth of flavour. It is also an excellent addition to marinades.

Aubergine (eggplant) is often dull-looking when steamed. To satisfy the Chinese need for effective presentation, serve it in a plain sandpot or small casserole or decorate the dish with herbs and raw vegetables such as carved radishes and carrots.

Pork Spare Ribs with Black Beans

Serves 4–5 with other dishes and rice

1 kg/2¼ lb small spare ribs

12 red dates

1 tbsp black beans, soaked in hot water for 10 minutes

2 tsp rock sugar or granulated sugar

2 tbsp light soy sauce

1 tbsp vegetable or peanut oil

1 tbsp cornflour (cornstarch)

Easy to prepare and delicious to eat, these subtly flavoured ribs are a healthy alternative to the marinated and sticky deep-fried versions common in Chinese restaurants.

Place the ribs and dates in a heatproof dish. Drain the black beans and gently press and mix them with the remaining ingredients, adding a tablespoon of water.

Pour the sauce over the ribs and dates. Cover the dish with foil and place in a preheated steamer; steam vigorously for 1 hour.

Our Secret
A mellow sweet and slightly tart fruity flavour is a perfectly Chinese complement for pork, far preferable to the eponymous and overdone sweet and sour, developed for the foreign palate. Stoned fresh plums are also traditional, but once you know the correct combination of flavours you can experiment with many soft fruits (small fruit without pits), adding more or less sugar to taste.

Mantou

Steaming wheat dough produces a light spongy bun, good for dipping in soups and mopping up sauces and gravy. These are eaten every day in Northern China, especially at lunch time. They look and taste beautiful when set against colourful and savoury stir fried dishes.

Dissolve the yeast in 2 tablespoons of warm water and set aside in a warm place for 15 minutes. Sift the flour into a large bowl and stir in the sugar and salt.

Make a well in the centre and pour in the dissolved yeast and 250ml/8 fl oz/1 cup warm water. Stir until the dough comes away from the sides. Press and knead on a floured surface for 5 minutes, dusting with flour if necessary. Work in the oil. The dough should be soft and springy.

Cover the dough and set aside to rise in a warm place for about 2 hours until doubled in size.

Turn the dough out on to a floured surface and shape into a rectangle.

Sprinkle evenly with the baking powder and then fold in half and knead again for 5 minutes, dusting with flour when necessary.

Divide the dough in half, then roll into two 18 cm/7 in sausages. Cut each sausage into six pieces and place well-spaced on a baking sheet (cookie sheet). Cover and set aside again for 40 minutes or until they double in size.

Place the buns on a damp cloth over a heatproof dish in a steamer and steam over fast boiling water for 15 minutes. Turn the heat off and leave to cool before removing. Repeat until all the buns are fully cooked.

Makes 12

15 g/½ oz dry yeast

500 g/1 lb plain (all-purpose) flour

1 tbsp rock or granulated sugar

pinch of salt

1 tbsp vegetable or peanut oil

1 tsp baking powder

Our Secret

Mantou don't keep very well. After a day or two you can reconstitute them by toasting, griddling, dry or deep-frying them or simply replacing them in the steamer for a few minutes. To dry-fry, toast or griddle, cut them into slices.

Chicken Steamed in Lotus Leaves

Serve 4

3 tbsp glutinous rice

3 pieces of lotus leaf

1.3–1.6 kg/3–3½ lb chicken

2 tbsp dark soy sauce

vegetable oil for deep-frying

2 medium onions, chopped

2 spring onions (scallions), chopped

6 tbsp drained, chopped winter pickle

2 tbsp *Shaoxing* (rice) wine or medium sherry

salt to taste

This is a recipe passed down through our family. The flesh of the chicken is tender, but the lotus and winter pickle (dong cai) give even the most tasteless bird a dramatic flavour. If you are a chilli lover, swap the winter pickle for the knobbly Sichuan pickle (zha cai) which can be put whole into the cavity of the chicken. Served in a bamboo steamer with the leaves draped over the edges this makes a handsome central dish. Serve with rice and stir fried dishes that have plenty of sauce.

Soak the rice in cold water for 20 minutes, then drain. Soak the lotus leaves in warm water for 15 minutes. Drain.

Bring a pan of water to the boil and add the chicken. Simmer for 5 minutes. Drain and pat the chicken dry with a clean cloth. Pull away the skin and discard.

Rub the chicken all over with the soy sauce. Heat enough oil in the wok to come half-way up the chicken. When the oil is hot enough to brown a cube of bread, slowly lower the chicken in, turning it over and basting until brown all over. Carefully lift it out and set it on a wire rack to drain.

Meanwhile mix the onions and spring onions with the pickle, rice, *Shaoxing* wine and salt. Stuff the chicken with this mixture, then wrap the chicken in the soaked lotus leaves and place in the steamer. Steam for 2½ hours.

Serve by bringing the steamer to the table and unwrapping the chicken at the table. Then just loosen the flesh from the bone, and spoon out some of the stuffing from the cavity, and let your guests help themselves.

Our Secret
It would be traditional to brown the chicken in rendered lard, but a modern alternative would be to use butter which gives a rich, although not very Chinese flavour. The effect of deep-frying is simply to colour and flavour the skin. The flesh of the chicken is light and aromatic from the long steaming and makes a fine contrast to other more heavily spiced dishes.

Cucumber Boats

Steamed cucumber retains its refreshing flavour while the flesh softens to the consistency of a firm melon. Stuffed with pork and prawns (shrimp) and served with a light parsley sauce, these steamed cucumber boats make a light and healthy supper dish that you can prepare in under 30 minutes.

Finely mince the ginger, spring onion and fresh prawns (shrimp) and mix evenly into the pork. Add all of the remaining ingredients, except the cornflour (cornstarch) and cucumber. Dust the inside of the cucumber with cornflour and spoon the stuffing into the cavity. Cut the cucumber halves into 5 cm/2 in sections. Place in a heatproof dish, cover and steam for 20 minutes. Reserve the cooling liquid.

When the cucumbers have steamed thoroughly, prepare the sauce. Heat the oil in the wok. When hot, turn the spring onion and flat-leaf parsley in the oil briefly and then pour on the liquid from the steamed cucumbers. Add the soy sauce, wine and sesame oil and stir over a high heat to reduce quickly.

Drizzle the sauce over the cucumbers to serve.

Serve 4

1 slice fresh root ginger

1 spring onion (scallion)

100 g/3½ oz fresh prawns, shelled (shrimp)

120 g/4 oz/½ cup lean pork, finely minced

½ tsp salt

½ tbsp light soy sauce

½ tsp rock or granulated sugar

pinch of pepper

2 tbsp vegetable or peanut oil

2 tsp cornflour (cornstarch), dissolved in a little water

2 large cucumbers, halved horizontally, skin and seeds removed

For the sauce:

3 tbsp vegetable or peanut oil

1 spring onion (scallion), finely chopped

2 large handfuls flat leaf parsley, roughly chopped

2 tbsp light soy sauce

4 tbsp *Shaoxing* (rice) wine or medium sherry

2 tbsp sesame oil

Our Secret

You can stuff cucumbers with any finely minced meat. Pork is the most traditional, but chicken or beef are equally good. As a family we are partial to lamb, but Chinese cooks tend to feel that the strong flavour of lamb meat needs an equally strong flavour to balance it, so add a little garlic and fresh coriander (cilantro) to the stuffing.

Steamed Eggs with Prawns (Shrimp)

Serves 2 as a side dish

2 eggs

300 ml/10fl oz/1¼ cups
good-quality cold chicken
stock

salt and pepper to taste

3 tbsp peeled prawns,
(shrimp) deveined

2 tbsp cooked peas

1 tbsp light soy sauce

1 spring onion (scallion),
chopped

At its most basic, this dish consists of no more than eggs mixed with stock then steamed for about 15 minutes until it sets. Finely chopped spring onion (scallion) is then scattered over the surface.

Beat the eggs and mix in the stock. Season with salt and pepper. Stir in half the prawns (shrimp) and all the peas and put in an attractive heatproof dish. Place in a steamer, cover and steam for 15 minutes.

Arrange the remaining prawns (shrimp) on top, pour the soy sauce over and steam for a further 4 minutes.

Sprinkle the chopped spring onion over to serve.

Our Secret
Serve this plainly with fewer peas and prawns (shrimp) to someone who is convalescing and needs something simple and nutritious. At home this dish was often served up in one of our English grandmother's porcelain egg poachers. If you have several of these it would make a very attractive arrangement for one small course at a dinner party.

Bao Zi Dumplings

Steamed dumplings are staple fare all over China. Because, or despite the fact they have always been an integral part of school lunches, they are held in great affection. Together with a noodle soup dish they make a filling and nutritious lunch.

Mix the yeast with 4 tablespoons of warm water and 1 teaspoon of sugar. Leave to stand until it froths. Sift the flour and remaining sugar into a bowl and make a well in the centre. Pour in the yeast mixture with 250 ml/8fl oz/1 cup warm water. Mix and knead the dough. Leave in a warm place until doubled in size.

Meanwhile, prepare the filling. In a large bowl, combine the soy sauce, salt, sugar, pepper, and 2 tablespoons of water. Add the pork and marinate for 30 minutes.

Wash the cabbage and blanch whole in a saucepan of boiling water for 30 seconds. Squeeze the cabbage dry and chop into small pieces. Mix the mushrooms and cabbage together with the minced pork. Heat the vegetable oil in a pan and add the meat mixture. Stir fry all together for 4 minutes, then sprinkle with sesame oil. Leave the filling on one side to cool.

Knead the dough well, then leave to rise in a warm place until about half the size again. Take a handful of dough and knead for a minute or two. Roll out the dough into about 20 6 cm/2½ in flat rounds. Place about 1 tablespoon of meat filling on each round. Gather up the edges and pinch to cover the filling.

Steam for 12 minutes, keeping the individual dumplings apart.

Makes about 20

15 g/½ oz dry yeast

1 tbsp rock or granulated sugar

400 g/14 oz/3½ cups self-raising (self-rising) flour

For the filling:

2 tbsp light soy sauce

1 tsp salt

1 tsp rock or granulated sugar

½ tsp pepper

500 g/1 lb/2 cups minced pork

1 Chinese cabbage

6 Chinese dried mushrooms, soaked in warm water for 30 minutes, hard stalks removed and caps finely chopped

2 tbsp vegetable or peanut oil

2 tsp sesame oil

Our Secrets
Sometimes a chunk of roast pork is used to fill the dumplings.

You can use honey roast pork, which gives the dumplings their characteristic savoury sweetness. Chopped nuts and sesame seeds are often fried in pork fat to make a nutty filling.

At a festival or holiday, sweet and savoury may be distinguished by marking the sweet dumplings with a red dot. To make a sweet filling, form the dough into a shell shape and fill with 2 teaspoons of sweet red bean paste.

Deep-frying and Double Cooking

Steaming and sizzling

Double cooking combines at least two different techniques; steamed food, prepared with the plainest and most simple technique, is often given a rich and flamboyant finish by plunging it into hot oil.

Occasionally deep-frying is an end in itself (see Dry-Tossed Chilli Prawns (Shrimp) or Chicken Chilli Mountain which are deep-fried first and then dry tossed together with chilli). But usually there is a preliminary steaming, stewing or marinating before the final hot oil shock.

The secret of Chinese deep-frying is in marinating in different spices and sauces and altering the intensity of the heat to create a variety of final textures to a dish (see Fish Salad with Star Anise). To get the best flavours out of deep-frying, the meat or seafood should be marinated or sometimes pre-cooked in salt, wine or soy sauce. Deep-frying in two stages allows the food to have a resting period when it cooks in its own heat and lets moisture evaporate. Thus the surface is made especially crisp during the second fry.

It is possible to deep fry in a wok, fish kettle or large pan. For most recipes the oil must be so hot it begins to ripple (when a piece of bread foams instantly it is ready) and it must be deep enough that it covers the ingredients and so that the temperature does not reduce too much when the food is added, otherwise the result will be oily.

Combined, these two techniques create the most extraordinary dishes (see Crispy Sichuan Duck or Crispy Lamb Wrapped in Lettuce). They are also easy to prepare in advance.

Dry-tossed Chilli Prawns (Shrimp)

An elegant and tasty way to start a meal, these can be served with one or two other dishes. Quick to prepare, and simple to serve, they are also ideal as finger food for a cocktail party.

Place the prawns in a dish with the wine and leave to marinate for 10 minutes.

Heat the oil in a wok until it just begins to smoke. Add the prawns and deep-fry for just a few seconds until they just change colour. Then quickly remove with a slotted spoon and drain on kitchen paper (paper towels). Pour off the oil.

Heat the wok again and add the prawns, garlic, chilli and spring onion. Toss together for 1 minute. Sprinkle with salt and pepper and turn together once more. Serve immediately garnished with finely chopped chilli.

Serves 4 as a starter

270 g/9 oz tiger prawns in their shells, heads and tails removed

1½ tsp *Shaoxing* (rice) wine or medium sherry

vegetable oil, for deep-frying

2 cloves garlic, crushed and finely chopped

1 red chilli, seeded and finely sliced

1 large spring onion (scallion), chopped

pinch of salt

pinch of pepper

finely chopped chilli to garnish

Our Secret
For a glazed coating reduce the marinade in the wok till it goes sticky, then pour over the prawns. Remember that this is not good for finger food though.

Home-style Bean Curd

Serves 4–5

30 g/1 oz wood ear

500 g/1 lb/2 cups broccoli

1 cake of firm bean curd, cut into 5 cm x 2.5 cm x 1 cm/2 in x 1 in x ½ in pieces

oil for deep-frying

2 slices fresh root ginger, roughly chopped

2 cloves garlic, roughly chopped

2 spring onions (scallions), cut lengthways then into 2.5 cm/1 in pieces

75 ml/2½ fl oz/⅓ cup enhanced stock (see page 147)

1 tbsp light soy sauce

½ tsp hot bean paste or chilli sauce

1 tbsp hoisin sauce

1½ tsp oyster sauce

1 tsp each salt and sugar

2 tbsp *Shaoxing* (rice) wine or medium sherry

2 tsp sesame oil

Crunchy broccoli is particularly good with this kind of puffy, deep-fried bean curd. When deep-frying, adjust the cooking time according to how crunchy you like your bean curd.

Soak the wood ear overnight in warm water, drain and cut into strips. Break the broccoli into florets, halving the larger ones, and trim the thickest stems. Deep-fry the bean curd pieces in hot oil for about 15 minutes, until they puff up and turn golden.

Heat the wok and add 2½ tablespoons of oil. When hot, add the ginger, garlic, spring onions and broccoli and turn together for 2 minutes. Pour in the stock and sauces, salt, sugar and wine and bring to the boil.

Add the wood ear and toss gently for 1 minute. Reduce the heat, add the bean curd and simmer gently for another minute or so as the sauce reduces. If there is too much sauce, pour it off and reduce separately to avoid over-cooking the vegetables. Glaze with sesame oil before serving.

Our Secret

There are as many home-style bean curds as there are households in China. People sometimes use plain, boiled bean curd to avoid deep-frying techniques, or add extra chilli for more of a kick.

Chicken Chilli Mountain

This is not for the faint hearted. The little chunks of chicken leg nestle inside a great mountain of fiery red chillies. Don't serve this alone unless you want to shock your guests – you can't eat very much at one time! To show this dish off to best effect, serve it with a very plain steamed dish such as Steamed Fish in Lotus Leaves (see page 45) and a green vegetable and rice.

Remove the skin from the chicken. Chop each leg into bite-size pieces. Give all the meat a good bash with the side of a chopper to loosen up the grain. Chop the breast into bite-size pieces. Sprinkle with a pinch of salt and the Sichuan peppercorns. Mix in the beaten egg white and the cornflour, stirring until smooth. Marinate for about 30 minutes.

Heat the wok, then add the oil. When it just begins to smoke, gently lower in the chicken pieces and deep-fry for 2½ minutes until light brown. Move the pieces around to prevent sticking. Scoop out the chicken and set aside. Pour away the oil. (If the flour has stuck in the wok give it a scrub.)

Heat the wok again with 1 tablespoon of oil. Toss in the chilli peppers and turn gently in the oil for 30 seconds. Then add the ginger, onions and chicken, stirring to prevent sticking. Immediately pour in the sugar, a pinch of salt, vinegar, soy sauce, *Shaoxing* wine and stock. When the liquid boils, cover and simmer until almost dry, stirring from time to time to prevent sticking. Drizzle with sesame oil.

Finally stir together and pour into a hot serving dish, arranging the chilli in a mountain so that your guests have to root around for the chicken within.

Our Secret
You can control how hot this dish is by selecting the chilli peppers carefully. Fat, red ones are milder than the long, thin devils.

Serves 4 with rice and another one or two dishes

500 g/1 lb chicken legs and/or breasts

salt

½ tsp Sichuan peppercorns, roasted and crushed

1 beaten egg white

2 tsp cornflour (cornstarch)

vegetable oil for deep-frying

500 g/1 lb whole red chilli peppers, with stalks

4 slices fresh root ginger, finely minced

1 large spring onion (scallion) or 1 small onion, finely chopped

2 tsp rock or granulated sugar

1 tbsp *Zhengjiang*, red wine or balsamic vinegar

1 tbsp dark soy sauce

1 tbsp *Shaoxing* (rice) wine or medium sherry

2 tbsp reduced stock

2 tsp sesame oil

deep-frying and double frying 59

Crispy Lamb Wrapped in Lettuce

Serves 4 as one whole course with rice and a couple of dishes to follow

360 g/12 oz breast of lamb

4 slices fresh root ginger, shredded

4 cloves garlic, crushed and finely chopped

5 spring onions (scallions), shredded and finely chopped

3 tsp dry-roasted and pounded Sichuan peppercorns

1 tbsp salt

3 tbsp dark soy sauce

1 tsp five-spice powder

2 tbsp *Shaoxing* (rice) wine or medium sherry

vegetable oil for deep-frying

For serving:

iceberg lettuce leaves and/or pancakes (see page 113)

sweet yellow bean sauce or hoisin sauce (see page 121)

shredded cucumber and spring onions to serve

This is a big dish that should be served as one course on its own. It is adapted from those barbecued lamb dishes that evoke the smoky flavours of cooking over an open fire on the Steppes. You may need someone to help you as deep-frying, especially in a round-bottomed wok, can be a perilous business.

Ask your butcher to cut the bone away from the meat. Then remove the skin. Mix the ginger, garlic and spring onions with the peppercorns and salt and rub into the lamb.

Combine the soy sauce, five-spice powder and wine. Place in a bowl with the lamb and marinate overnight. Discard the peppercorns.

Place the lamb in a heatproof bowl and cover with foil. Steam in a covered pan for 2 hours. Leave to cool.

When required, make sure the wok is properly stabilised, preferably on a proper wok ring. Heat the wok until it is very hot, pour in the oil and wait 10–15 seconds. When the oil is almost smoking, lower in the lamb slowly and carefully and deep-fry for 4 minutes. Turn it once to make sure both sides brown evenly, basting the top continuously.

Remove from the oil and leave on a rack so that the meat is thoroughly drained. Chop roughly into small pieces for wrapping in lettuce. Alternatively, serve inside pancakes with sweet yellow bean sauce (see pages 121), shredded cucumber and spring onions.

Our Secrets

Long-steaming the meat makes it very tender, while the outside is golden brown. If you are short of time, steam the lamb first and set aside, then all that is needed is the final deep-fry for a few minutes.

For large cuts of meat, use a heavy deep pan that will hold a lot of oil without burning it. You can use a wok, soup kettle, roasting pan or enameled casserole. To get the temperature of the oil just right, heat the pan first and leave the oil until it begins to move on the surface and generates a fair amount of heat to the hand. A piece of bread thrown into the oil will sizzle instantly.

Guo-ta Fish Omelette

This dish is a family favourite and was always on the menu in our family restaurants. It is very quick and easy.

Rub the fish with salt, pepper and sesame oil. Pour the eggs over the fish. Mix together the stock, soy sauce and wine.

Heat the wok and then add the oil. When it just begins to smoke, lay the fish into the oil. Then pour the beaten egg on top.

Cook over a medium heat for about 3 minutes, until the egg begins to set, giving it a little shake from time to time to prevent sticking. (To avoid burning the eggs on the bottom of the wok keep checking the colour underneath. If the bottom is well-cooked and the top still liquid, finish cooking under the grill.)

Sprinkle the shredded onions, garlic and ginger over the omelette. Pour the stock mixture over the top of the omelette. Bring to the boil and simmer for a further 4 minutes. Transfer the omelette to a well-heated serving dish.

Serves 2 with rice and a vegetable

2 medium fillets of plaice

pinch of salt

pepper to taste

1 tsp sesame oil

3 eggs, beaten

3 tbsp good-quality stock

1½ tsp light soy sauce

1½ tsp *Shaoxing* (rice) wine or medium sherry

3 tbsp vegetable or peanut oil

1½ spring onions (scallions), chopped into thin shreds lengthways

1 large clove garlic, finely sliced

2 slices fresh root ginger, shredded

Our Secrets

Fresh fish is obviously preferable for this dish, but it is also easy with frozen fillets. You simply need to cook them for a little longer.

The combination of garlic, ginger and spring onions makes a classic dressing for fish dishes, whether steamed or stir fried. They are thought to neutralise any unpleasant fishiness, while not spoiling the natural flavour.

Crispy Sichuan Duck

Serves 4

1 medium-sized duck, about 2 kg/4½ lb

2½ tbsp salt

1 tsp Sichuan peppercorns

1 tsp five-spice powder

large head of fresh root ginger

4 large spring onions (scallions) or 2 leeks, roughly chopped

1 tbsp dark soy sauce

1 tbsp yellow bean sauce

flour for sprinkling

oil for deep-frying

For serving:

Chinese pancakes (see page 113)

cucumber and spring onions

sweet yellow bean sauce or hoisin sauce (see page 121)

Crispy Sichuan duck is one of those big dishes that makes the centrepiece of many modern restaurant menus. It takes a while to prepare, but it is not very labour intensive. The marinating can be done overnight, but you will need to steam the duck for 3 hours in a large steamer, then let it cool. All of this can be done well in advance. Serve this as a separate course of a banquet after the cold hors d'oeuvre and before the rice and noodle dishes.

Cut out the duck tail and the oil glands just inside the tail end. Rinse the duck and pat dry, then flatten the duck by pressing down sharply on its breast bone.

Dry-fry the salt and Sichuan peppercorns gently for 5 minutes, stirring, then crush to a fine powder. Mix with the five-spice powder and rub well into the duck's skin. Cut the ginger into fine slices and cover the duck with them. Marinate overnight.

Pour off any liquid that has collected under the duck. Stuff it with the onions and place in a heatproof dish in a steamer. Steam vigorously for 3 hours.

When cool, remove the onions and pat the duck dry. Mix the soy sauce and yellow bean sauce and brush the skin, finishing with a fine coating of flour.

Heat the oil in a wok or fish kettle until very hot. Carefully slip the duck into the oil and sizzle for about 10 minutes basting continuously and turning once. Remove the duck when the skin is a deep crisp golden brown. Drain the duck on a rack, then scrape away the flesh from the bones. To serve spread the pancakes with a little bean or hoisin sauce. Top with a pile of shredded cucumber and spring onions, then a little of the duck and a piece of skin and roll up.

Our Secrets

You should lower the duck very slowly into the oil to prevent it cooling suddenly. Cooled oil will slow down the process and make the skin greasy and unpleasant. A short, sharp deep-fry will give a lovely crispy skin.

For quick roast duck with a Chinese feel, rub the skin with soy sauce and a thin layer of honey. Then roast directly on the oven shelf with a drip pan on the shelf below.

Fish Salad with Star Anise

The delicate white flesh of the fish combined with the rich taste of soy and aniseed make this a feast of dramatic flavours. Set against the rich, fresh green of the salad and the red of radishes it is also a work of art.

Rub the fish with salt and pepper. (Do not remove the skin.) Place the onions and star anise in a flat-bottomed pan, then add the soy sauce, sugar, wine, ginger and stock. Place the fish, skin side up, in the pan and marinate for 2 hours. Remove the fish and set aside.

Turn the heat on under the pan and bring to the boil. Add the fish and simmer for 15 minutes, turning the fish once, and basting until the liquid thickens.

Turn the heat off and leave to marinate for a further hour. Remove the fish from the marinade and leave to drain on a rack before you complete the last stage.

Deep fry the fish for 2½ minutes, skin side down. Remove carefully and drain away excess oil. When the fish has cooled cut it into 2.5 cm/1 in slices and arrange in the centre of a bed of green leaves. Garnish with sliced radishes and drizzle with sesame oil.

Serves 2 as a starter

2 medium fillets of haddock

1½ tsp salt

pinch pepper

2 medium onions, finely sliced

4 pieces star anise

4 tbsp dark soy sauce

1½ tbsp rock or granulated sugar

2 tbsp *Shaoxing* (rice) wine or medium sherry

3 slices fresh root ginger, shredded

6 tbsp good-quality chicken or fish stock

oil for deep-frying

green leaves, such as lamb's lettuce or young spinach, and radishes to garnish

4 tsp sesame oil

Our Secret

When deep-frying steamed or braised fish or meat it is important to cool and drain each piece carefully. Wet and juicy pieces will spit and fail to get a crispy finish.

Crispy Five-spice Chicken Legs

Serves 4

8 chicken drumsticks

2½ tsp salt

pepper to taste

1 tsp ground ginger

vegetable oil for
deep-frying

For the sauce:

300 ml/10 fl oz/1¼ cups
enhanced chicken stock
(see page 145)

1½ tbsp hoisin sauce

1½ tbsp yellow bean paste

¾ tsp white pepper

1½ tbsp whole five-spice

*The combination of five-spice, hoisin and yellow bean sauce gives
this dish a full-blooded savouriness. The preparation may seem fiddly,
but the beauty is that it can be done in advance, leaving the deep-
frying for the last minute.*

Rub the chicken drumsticks with a mixture of salt, pepper and
ground ginger.

Leave to season marinade for 30 minutes.

Bring a pan of water to the boil, add the drumsticks and boil for three
minutes. Drain and cool.

Place the sauce ingredients in a wok or pan and bring to the boil.

Add the part-cooked drumsticks. Bring back to the boil and simmer
for about 15 minutes. Leave the drumsticks to cool in the sauce for a
further 15 minutes, then remove and dry thoroughly. (Store them
overnight in the refrigerator if necessary.)

When you are about to eat, heat the oil in a wok or deep-fat fryer.
When hot (a cube of bread should sizzle when you drop it in), gently
fry the chicken for about 5 minutes, until golden-brown.

Take the chicken out of the pan, remove the knuckle from the
drumstick and arrange the legs on a heated plate around a dish of
Sweet Yellow Bean Sauce (see page 121).

Our Secret
These chicken legs are perfect finger food for a buffet party served
hot or cold.

Bean Curd with Mushrooms

Vegetarian friends will love this substantial supper dish. The deep-fried bean curd is rich and savoury, while the mushrooms make a beautiful contrast to the fresh, crisp carrot and mangetout.

Soak the mushrooms in hot water for 30 minutes, remove the hard stalks and quarter the caps. Heat the oil for deep-frying in a pan until it begins to smoke. Add the bean curd and deep-fry for about 10 minutes, or until it turns golden brown. Remove with a slotted spoon and set aside.

Heat the 3 tbsp oil in a wok until it begins to smoke. Add the garlic, onion and mushrooms. Stir fry for 2 minutes before adding the remaining vegetables.

Add the stock and the bean curd. Flavour with the soy and oyster sauces. Bring to the boil, turning continuously, and then simmer and reduce for 2 minutes until the sauce thickens a little. Add the pepper, wine and sesame oil and turn for a few more seconds.

Stir in the blended cornflour to thicken the sauce. Garnish with radishes and spring onions.

Serves 4

10 large Chinese dried mushrooms

vegetable oil for deep-frying

20 pieces of firm bean curd, 2.5 cm/1 in square and 1 cm/½ in thick

3 tbsp vegetable or peanut oil

6 cloves garlic, crushed and finely chopped

½ medium Spanish onion, finely sliced

1 small carrot, finely sliced

60 g/2 oz mangetout

200 ml/7 fl oz/scant 1 cup hot vegetable stock

1 tbsp dark soy sauce

1 tbsp oyster sauce, preferably vegetarian

pinch of pepper

1 tbsp *Shaoxing* (rice) wine or medium sherry

t tsp sesame oil

1 tsp cornflour (cornstarch) blended with water

shredded pink radishes and finely sliced spring onions (scallions) to garnish (optional)

Our Secret
The crisp, golden chunks of bean curd are a delight in themselves and often do not make it to the second stage in our household, having been scavenged by the children. To dress them simply for a finger snack to go with wine, dry-fry them with a little chilli and salt.

Salads and
Vegetarian Dishes

Dishes for every occasion

All the dishes in this chapter can be served as vegetarian or also demi-vegetarian starters to a banquet. Most can also be served in greater quantity as a main or side dish, or in the case of pickles, a rich Chinese tradition, as a 'condiment' to a soup. In Northern and Eastern China hors d'oeuvres would be served cold, typically a cold platter made up of pickles and small cured meats served in aspic. The latter are often connoisseur foods, as are the hot tossed mixtures favoured by southerners made up of duck tongues, offal and chicken's feet.

Since the diet of the average Chinese has always been basically vegetarian with the odd scattering of sliced or minced meat, there are a multitude of dishes to chose from for this chapter. You can use vegetables of different textures and colours to personalise your own starter. We suggest Red Braised Mushrooms, any of the Pickles, Chilli French Beans and Dry Tossed Chilli Prawns. You could also use the Bread Fish, Spring Onion Cakes and Mantou (see Rice and Breads chapter) to interesting effect.

We can adapt Chinese hors d'oeuvre to our own way of eating. In every Chinese city there is a maze of small streets where people promenade in the evenings. Here the pavement will be lined with tiny stalls each with its own hob or griddle serving specialist fare, often characteristically Hunanese, Chaozhou or Sichuan. This way of eating explodes on to the street at New Year and at the temple fairs, where you will find dan dan noodles, fried milk, rice cakes, gruels and sweet congees, deep-fried bean curd, and every kind of barbecued food stuck on a stick.

We have selected some of these dishes to pick at in the evening or to help the wine go down at a party. But for the most part this chapter describes practical dishes that you might simply use as an alternative to a plain green salad or side vegetable and can serve with a selection of stir fried dishes or to complement a rich casserole.

Tomato and Cucumber Salad

Here is a way of dressing up tomato and cucumber salad so that you won't recognise it! The vinegar heightens the fresh crunchiness, while sesame oil gives it a lovely nutty flavour.

Sprinkle the tomatoes evenly with the salt. Leave to season for 30 minutes, then pour away any excess juices. Mix the tomato and cucumber pieces.

Combine the sugar, vinegar and oils and mix thoroughly. Pour over the salad and toss until well coated. Garnish with the mint or coriander leaves to serve.

Serves 4–5

210 g/7 oz cherry tomatoes, halved

1 tsp salt

1 medium cucumber, halved lengthways and cut into 5 mm/¼ in slices

1 tbsp rock or granulated sugar

2 tbsp rice or white wine vinegar

1 tbsp sunflower oil

1½ tbsp sesame oil

Thai mint or coriander (cilantro) leaves to garnish (optional)

Our Secret
This kind of salad can be served straight away, but left to marinate the dressing soaks into the cucumber and makes it increasingly savoury. So make lots and leave some overnight in the refrigerator.

Chilli French Beans

Serves 4 as a side dish

240 g/8 oz/1 cup French (green) beans, halved

1 tbsp vegetable or peanut oil

1 green or red chilli, seeded and finely chopped

2 whole cloves garlic

1 tbsp light soy sauce

½ tsp rock or granulated sugar

½ tsp sesame oil

French (green) beans hardly need to be dressed up in any way, but the chilli here adds a kick. Be careful not to choke when you throw the chillies into the hot oil!

Blanch the beans for 30 seconds, then drain. Refresh under cold water and drain again.

Heat the oil over a high heat and throw in the chilli to flavour the oil for 30 seconds. Then throw in the garlic. Turn in the oil and then immediately add the French beans. Add the soy sauce and sugar and stir fry for 3 minutes until well seasoned.

Sprinkle with sesame oil to serve.

Our Secret

French beans are a good deal finer and cook more quickly than their Chinese counterpart which need blanching. But they are a European improvement on the original dish. Keep the beans moving to stop them drying out: listen for a crackling sound and if the beans are not quite done add enough water or stock to keep the pan moist.

salads and vegetarian dishes

Bean Curd and Chive Salad

Soft bland bean curd gives a radical contrast to the pungent chives and the hot saltiness of the pickle in this dish. Serve this as a side salad on a summer's day. It is so spicy that a little goes a long way.

Mix the pickle, cabbage and chives with the oils, soy sauce, vinegar, sugar, garlic and wine. Leave to stand for 30 minutes. Arrange the bean curd on a serving dish. Spoon the sauce over the bean curd and serve.

Serves 6 as a side salad

1½ tbsp Sichuan pickle (*zha cai*), chopped

1½ tbsp preserved cabbage (snow pickle), chopped

120 g/4 oz/½ cup Chinese chives, or a mixture of coriander, spring onions and English chives, chopped

2½ tbsp vegetable oil

2½ tbsp sesame oil

2 tbsp dark soy sauce

3 tbsp rice or white wine vinegar

2 tsp rock or granulated sugar

2 cloves garlic, crushed and finely chopped

2 tbsp *Shaoxing* (rice) wine

210 g/7 oz silken bean curd, cut into 2.5 cm/ 1 in cubes

Our Secret

Many cooks have had disastrous encounters with bean curd, largely because they do not buy the right kind. The most fundamental distinction to make is between soft (silken) and firm (*doufu*). The former is often described as Japanese in Chinese supermarkets, even though it is very common in China where they sometimes make it from peanuts. It is generally sold in small cartons. Silken bean curd is the only bean curd that can be eaten raw with a dressing such as the recipe above, or sweet in combination with syrup. It must be used carefully in stir fry.

Spinach and Radish Salad

Serves 4 as a side salad

1 bunch large red radishes

1 tsp salt

1kg /2¼ lb tender young
spinach

2 tsp light soy sauce

1½ tsp caster sugar

3 tsp sesame oil

2 tsp rice or white wine
vinegar

pinch of pepper

*This is a favourite recipe of father's old friend Madame Fei, one of
those ageless and ever cheerful women who have a natural talent for
producing beautiful and flavoursome Chinese food. We have slightly
modified her recipe by reducing the salt and adding a little vinegar.*

Clean and trim the radishes. Flatten with the side of a cleaver or
with a meat tenderiser. Sprinkle with salt and leave to sweat for a
few minutes.

Clean the spinach, remove all the tough stalks and discoloured
leaves. Place the leaves into a saucepan and pour a kettle full of
boiling water over them. Strain immediately and rinse with cold water.
Strain away all the water and dry thoroughly. Chop the spinach.

Sprinkle the soy sauce, sugar, oil, vinegar and pepper over the
spinach and mix well. Arrange on a large platter and place the
salted radishes on the top.

Our Secrets
Giving crisp, juicy vegetables like radishes and cucumber a hard
slap with a chopper and then salting them allows the vegetables
to sweat away excess fluid and intensifies their natural flavour.

In this dish the combination of red radishes and green spinach
satisfies the Chinese need for bright and youthful vibrance. In
selecting dishes, balancing ingredients with a variety of colours
and textures is just as important as adjusting the flavour.

Sesame Cucumber and Daikon Salad

This is a crisp, raw salad with the nutty flavour of sesame. The daikon gives a clean sharp flavour which makes a refreshing contrast to the more savoury and rich stir fry or casserole dishes.

Slice the cucumber in half lengthways and then into half-moons about 5 mm/¼ in thick. Cut them into quarters. Sprinkle with salt and sugar and leave in the refrigerator for 30 minutes. Squeeze and drain away any excess liquid.

Cut the daikon as the cucumber. Toss with sesame oil. Trim the thick stems from the watercress. Wash thoroughly and leave to dry. Place in a salad bowl and arrange the cucumber and daikon on top.

Serves 4 as a side salad

½ medium cucumber

½ tsp salt

½ tsp sugar

240 g/8 oz/1 cup daikon
(Chinese white radish)

1 tbsp sesame oil

1 bunch watercress

Our Secret
The beauty of daikon (literally translated as 'big root' because they can be nearly 60 cm/2 ft), Chinese white radish, or Japanese mooli, is that it can be wrapped in foil and kept in the refrigerator for several weeks. In addition to salads, it makes a very tasty addition to any soup stock, both meat or vegetarian, stir fry or casserole.

Bak Choy with Bean Curd

Serves 2

3 tbsp vegetable or peanut oil

2 cloves garlic, crushed and chopped

1 tsp red fermented bean curd

250 g/9 oz/1 cup bak choy, leaves and white stems cut into short strips 4 cm/1½ in wide, or 400 g/14 oz spinach, thick stalks removed

1 tbsp good-quality stock

pinch of salt

½ tsp rock or granulated sugar

Bak choy is a tremendously versatile and attractive vegetable. Green cabbage can also be used in the recipe below, but increase the cooking time a little. The red fermented bean curd can be omitted; replace it with 1 tablespoon of dark soy sauce. Children, who may find boiled greens inedible, are often converted by the addition of the garlic, a little soy sauce and oil.

Heat the oil in the wok, swirling it around until it starts to smoke. Add the garlic and red bean curd and crush together. Then add the white part of the bak choy or all of the spinach. Stir fry for 30 seconds, then turn down the heat.

Add the remaining green part of the bak choy with the stock, salt and sugar, then turn up the heat as high as possible, turning together for a further 1 minute.

Serve as a side dish with rice or add oiled noodles at the last stage and garnish with coriander (cilantro) for a good lunch.

Our Secret
Most Chinese fast food establishments simply blanch bak choy, mustard greens, Chinese leaves or other greens in boiling water for a second before turning them in hot oil with some oyster sauce and garlic for 30 seconds. The result is very good! Simply tailor the cooking time to how tough the greens are, but be careful not to overcook.

salads and vegetarian dishes

Shredded Vegetables

This is one of Nanny Ding's favourite dishes – a common home-style dish that you can serve at any time. The secret is to make sure the vegetables are cut very thinly and evenly and that the oil is very hot.

Heat the wok gently, then add the oil, heating over a low heat. Add the Sichuan peppercorns and turn slowly in the oil until they darken, but do not allow them to burn. Discard the peppercorns.

Turn up the heat and toss in the potato and carrot, turning them in the oil.

Stir fry for 4 minutes, turning every now and then to coat in the oil and prevent sticking – they should begin to brown a little.

Add the pepper and stir together for a further 1 minute. Make sure everything is heated through, then add the vinegar and soy sauce. Sprinkle over the salt and keep turning for a further 1 minute, making sure the vegetables do not become soggy.

Serves 4 as a side dish

3 tbsp vegetable or peanut oil

2 tsp Sichuan peppercorns (optional)

2 large potatoes, peeled and julienned into matchsticks

2 carrots, peeled and julienned into matchsticks

1 medium green or red (bell) pepper, cored, seeded and julienned into matchsticks

2 tbsp *Zhengjiang*, red wine or balsamic vinegar

2 tbsp light soy sauce

2 tsp salt

Our Secret

The secret of this dish is in the cutting of the vegetables. It is essential to julienne to a matchstick size so that the potatoes cook properly. In general, the key to successful stir frying of vegetables is to know the consistency of each vegetable and to adjust the fineness, cooking time and moment of assembly to suit.

Kelp and Celery Salad

Serves 4–6

60 g/2 oz kelp, soaked in warm water overnight

60 g/2 oz wood ears, soaked in warm water overnight, rinsed and finely sliced

240 g/8 oz/1 cup celery, cut into 5 cm x 0.5 cm/2 in x ¼ in lengths, then boiled for 1 minute

2 tomatoes, skinned, sliced and shredded

1 tbsp light soy sauce

1 tbsp sesame oil

⅛ tsp salt

½ tsp rock or granulated sugar

1 tsp *Zhenjiang*, red wine or balsamic vinegar

Kelp is rich in minerals, especially iodine, and thought to be a cooling, Yin food. Healing properties aside, this salad is also fresh, clean and crunchy, and makes a lovely lunch when served with one other dish.

Drain the kelp, place in a pan of boiling water and simmer for 4 hours.

Drain the kelp and slice it finely. Place the kelp, wood ears, celery and tomatoes in a bowl.

Mix together the soy sauce, sesame oil, salt, sugar and vinegar. Pour over the vegetables and toss well.

Our Secret
This is a traditional Chinese seaweed recipe using the same seaweed harvested from the Irish sea. The 'seaweed' normally sold in Chinese restaurants is a Chinese illusion prepared especially for the British public; the secret is to take the tough, dry outside leaves of spring greens, wash and dry thoroughly, roll up, slice extremely finely and deep-fry.

Broccoli in Oyster Sauce

The robust character of this nutritious vegetable makes a delicious dish when combined with the distinct flavour of oyster sauce (you can buy very good vegetarian versions). It takes only minutes to prepare and makes a tasty addition to any meal.

Bring a pan of water to the boil. Add the broccoli and simmer until it just begins to soften. Do not let it go soft. Drain and leave to dry.

Heat the butter or oil in a wok. When hot, add the broccoli and oyster sauce and turn together for 1 minute. Sprinkle on the wine and turn together until the liquid has reduced.

Serves 4 as a side dish

500 g/1 lb/2 cups broccoli, tough stems removed and broken into florets

40 g/1½ oz/3 tbsp butter or 2 tbsp vegetable oil

2 tbsp oyster sauce

2 tbsp *Shaoxing* (rice) wine

Our Secrets

Traditionally, oyster sauce is made from seasoned, dried oysters and gives a strong, savoury flavour. In our restaurant we use a vegetarian version which is just as good and is an invaluable addition to stir fried vegetarian dishes and bean curd casseroles.

In China, the hard stems of the broccoli are just as prized, if not more so, than the florets. Our chefs often slice them thickly and throw away the florets.

Red-braised Mushrooms

Serves 4

120 g/4 oz Chinese dried
mushrooms

3 tbsp vegetable or
peanut oil

1 slice fresh root ginger,
shredded

2 tbsp dark soy sauce

1 tbsp *Shaoxing* (rice) wine
or medium sherry

1 tbsp rock sugar or brown
sugar

1 tbsp sesame oil

*Served hot or cold, these red-braised Chinese mushrooms make a
rich and juicy appetiser or side dish. They also make a dark and
savoury contrast to crisper vegetables and cut meats on a cold platter.*

Soak the mushrooms in hot water for 30 minutes, then remove the
hard stalks and quarter the caps. Retain the soaking water.

Heat the wok, then add the oil. When it just begins to smoke scatter
in the mushrooms and ginger and turn together in the oil for
2 minutes. Add the soy sauce, wine, mushroom soaking water and
sugar, stirring together.

Bring to the boil, cover and simmer for 20 minutes or until most of
the liquid has been reduced and absorbed by the mushrooms. Glaze
with sesame oil to serve.

Our Secret
Rock sugar is a form of raw sugar which has a subtle, mellow
sweetness and coats red-cooked dishes with a shiny glaze. In most
good Chinese markets there is one stall piled high with these
crystalline rocks. To smash the rocks, wrap them first in a tea towel
and hit them with the back of a chopper or mallet. Otherwise they fly
all over the kitchen.

Nanny Ding's Peanut Salad

Nanny Ding was a one-woman wonder who cooked, cleaned and cared for the children. She came from a poor family and having raised three children herself was a marvel at making delicacies out of plain, rustic ingredients. This is a good substantial salad, with wonderful tastes and textures, served by nanny Ding last time we were in Beijing. It can be served on its own, with Mantou (see page 49) or any other bread, or simply with rice. It can also make up one of a number of different dishes to be served with rice.

Soak the bean curd for 30 minutes in hot, but not boiling water, then roughly tear it into thick shreds.

Bring a pan of water to the boil, then add the cauliflower and celery. Bring back to the boil and simmer gently for 5 minutes.

Meanwhile, heat the oil until it smokes. Toss in the carrots and lotus root and turn in the oil for 30 seconds. Add the wood ear, well-strained bean curd, stock powder, sesame oil or paste, vinegar, soy sauce and wine. Bring to the boil and simmer until the liquid has reduced a little.

Strain the boiled vegetables and add to the dressing in the pan. Turn all the ingredients so that they get a good coating of the hot dressing.

Garnish with coriander (cilantro). Serve hot or cold.

Serves 4 as a main dish; more as a side salad

90 g/3 oz sheets or sticks of dry bean curd

1 small cauliflower, broken into small florets

2 sticks celery, cut into 4 cm/1½ in lengths, then halved

3 tbsp vegetable or peanut oil

2 medium carrots, thinly sliced on the diagonal

120 g/4 oz canned lotus root, cut into 5 mm/¼ in slices

15 g/½ oz wood ear, soaked overnight in warm water

2 tsp vegetable stock powder (bouillon) or equivalent

1 tbsp sesame oil or 2 tsp sesame paste

1 tbsp rice or white wine vinegar

1 tbsp light soy sauce

2 tbsp *Shaoxing* (rice) wine or medium sherry

60 g/2 oz peanuts, boiled for 10 minutes

chopped coriander (cilantro) to garnish

Our Secret

Nanny Ding will be delighted to know we have included her salad. She prepared it for my vegetarian mother-in-law's visit. We cannot give enough stress to the importance of colour and texture in Chinese cuisine. Nanny Ding's salad is a gorgeous assembly of pale creams, browns and oranges framed with curly wood ear and crowned with the fresh green coriander (cilantro). The wood ear and bean curd sticks are also shiny, while the lotus root adds a wheel pattern to the final picture.

Stir Fried Cauliflower

*Serves 4 as one of a
number of dishes*

2 tbsp vegetable or
peanut oil

1 medium cauliflower,
broken into small florets
with slits in the thick stems

1 tsp salt

6 tbsp vegetarian stock

1 tbsp white wine vinegar

3 tbsp *Shaoxing* (rice) wine
or medium sherry

sesame oil to glaze

You will never again be able to eat plain boiled cauliflower!

Heat the wok and add the oil. When it just begins to smoke add the
cauliflower and toss quickly to coat in the oil. Turn down the heat to
medium and keep turning for 30 seconds.

Sprinkle in the salt and then add the stock, vinegar and wine. Bring
to the boil, cover, then simmer vigorously for 4 minutes. Finally, boil
off any remaining liquid and toss in a few drops of sesame oil to
glaze before serving.

Our Secret
Here we have a fast stir fry, followed by a short steam in stock,
vinegar and wine. This method beats blanching the vegetables first,
since with blanching you are always in danger of over-cooking,
especially with cauliflower. The beauty of this method is that the
cauliflower retains its colour and firmness while, at the same time,
becoming infused with savoury, piquant flavours.

White Fungus and Cucumber Salad

White fungus is thought to nourish the lungs, probably because its flowery texture looks a little like lung. It has a neutral taste, so it needs to be dressed with pungent and aromatic flavours.

Drain the white fungus, cut out the hard brown-yellow stem and discard. Tear the fungus into small pieces.

Pound the cucumber all along its length with the side of a chopper until it is distorted and half flattened. Cut it across into 2 cm/¾ in sections. Sprinkle with the salt and leave to drain in a colander for 10 minutes.

Toss the white fungus with the cucumber. Mix in the remaining ingredients except the coriander (cilantro) and toss well. Leave to marinate in the dressing for at least 1 hour in the refrigerator. Garnish with the coriander, to serve.

Serves 4 as one of a number of dishes

60 g/2 oz white fungus, soaked overnight

1 cucumber

1 tsp salt

3 cloves garlic, crushed and finely chopped

1 tbsp white wine vinegar

1 tbsp sesame oil

coriander (cilantro) to garnish

Our Secret

Make sure you buy a packet of white fungus with a good brilliant white colour. Many shops keep packages too long, so the petals begin to yellow. Added to a sweet soup with rock sugar, cassia and gingko nuts they look like a beautiful milky white flower.

Golden Dry-tossed Bean Curd

Serves 2

4 tbsp vegetable oil

360 g/12 oz firm bean curd, rinsed and left to dry, then cut into 2.5 cm x 4 cm/1 in x 1½ in squares.

2 tsp ground sea salt

1 spring onion (scallion), finely chopped

1 tbsp finely chopped chives for serving

1 bunch watercress, washed and roughly chopped, thick stems removed

For a simple and moreish starter, this dish is perfect with wine as an hors d'oeuvre (your guests will have to be adept with the chopsticks or small forks though).

Heat the wok and add the oil. When it has just begun to smoke gently, place the chunks of bean curd into the oil, browning them for 5 minutes on each side over a high heat. (Be careful not to smash the bean curd pieces.)

Add the salt and turn until the curd is golden. Add the spring onion and chives.

Stir once again. Remove from the oil using a slotted spoon and serve the bean curd on a bed of watercress.

Our Secrets

The amount of salt in this dish balances the oil and is characteristic of Sichuan cuisine – this is a dish to pick at with wine or as a starter so, like other finger food, it is meant to increase your thirst. For a fuller taste, add a dash of soy sauce, ground Sichuan pepper and oyster sauce or use a chilli or soy dip.

The bean curd referred to is the fresh, firm kind found in Chinese supermarkets, usually immersed in water in plastic cartons. If you are unsure what kind of bean curd you are using, poach it first. This both softens firm bean curd or firms up the soft, Japanese silken variety.

South Sea Salsa

Here is a recipe that belongs to our friend Jessica Khine, whose innovative twists on traditional oriental dishes are influenced by being Burmese, but having grown up in Japan and the UK. The idea of the salsa stems from the fact that in Burma all fried dishes come with a small side helping of onions smothered in some tangy sauce, chilli or otherwise, and wrapped in half a banana leaf. Serve it with the Vietnamese Vermicelli with Griddled Chicken (on page 94). Together they are light and perfect for a quick evening snack or a more substantial meal for lunch or dinner. They also go down very well at buffets as perfect fork food!

Drain the onions and toss with all the ingredients. Leave to chill in the refrigerator.

Serves 2–3 as a side salad

1 large red onion, thinly sliced and soaked in hot water for 2–3 hours

small fresh green chillies, according to taste

one handful of finely chopped coriander (cilantro) leaves and stems

salt, to taste

Thai fish sauce, to taste

grated zest and juice of 1 lime or lemon

grated cucumber or carrots, to garnish

Our Secret
Soaking the onion takes the sting out of it and makes it easy to consume in large quantities. The salsa has a good kick to it but, strangely, is much loved by those who are normally wary of very spicy food.

Radish and Carrot Pickle

*Serves 4 as a side
dish or starter*

500 g/1 lb carrots, sliced
into thin rounds

500 g/1 lb Chinese white
radish (daikon), sliced into
thin rounds

2 tsp salt

1 clove garlic

1 red chilli

2 tbsp fish sauce
(optional)

200 ml/7fl oz/scant 1 cup
rice vinegar or malt vinegar

100 g/3½ oz/scant 1 cup
granulated white sugar

Chinese chives to garnish

*There are many different kinds of pickles available canned or in jars.
Many, such as winter pickle, snow pickle or Sichuan pickle (zha cai)
are included in the recipes. They make a very good complement to
plain boiled rice and in a poor rural diet will often be all there is to
flavour the food. Here is a recipe for a quick pickle that should be
served as a starter or as one of the dishes in a banquet.*

Sprinkle the carrots and radish with the salt and leave for 30 minutes
until the vegetables become soft. Rinse thoroughly, then pat dry.

Crush the garlic and chop finely with the chilli, add to the vegetables.
Mix the remaining ingredients together with 900 ml/1½ pints/3¾ cups
water, then pour over the vegetables. Leave to pickle for 1 hour.
Serve with uncut Chinese chives trailing around the dish.

Our Secret
Any root vegetable can be pickled, and all traditional Chinese
kitchens will have a variety on hand. A standard brine would be
prepared from saline solution (4 tbsp salt to 2 litres/3½ pints/8½ cups
water) and 2 tablespoons of of alcohol (Father always used gin)
seasoned with dried chilli, Sichuan pepper and ginger. Some
vegetables can be sun-dried before pickling to deepen the flavour.

Bean Curd and Preserved Eggs

This is a deceptively rich dish that should be served with hot rice.

Cut each of the eggs into eight. Gently break up the bean curd and place on a dish. Sprinkle with salt and wine. Arrange the pieces of egg on top. Toss together before serving.

Serves 4 as a side dish or starter

2 preserved duck eggs, sold as *pi dan* (*pee dan*) in Chinese supermarkets

1 x 125 g carton silken bean curd

1 tsp salt

1 tbsp *Shaoxing* (rice) wine or medium sherry

Our Secret

Preserved eggs are generally available in Chinese supermarkets. In the old days we used to buy them covered in clay and straw, and were told that they had been buried for a hundred, or was that a thousand, years? Now they generally come clean and are a delicate duck-egg green. Inside the white has turned a translucent green-black and the yolk, just hard also has a deep greeny-black sheen – a colourful contrast with the silky white bean curd. You shouldn't try to eat too much *pi dan*, though the addition of wine, salt and plain silken bean curd neutralises their richness.

Noodle Dishes

How long are your noodles?

There are an indeterminate number of noodles, long ones, short ones, yellow ones, green ones, fat ones, thin ones, noodles made of wheat, eggs, flour, corn, rice, buckwheat or beans. Here's a guide to the main types used commonly in China.

Egg noodles come in many shapes and sizes: thick, fresh and oily like deep yellow oil noodles or thin and delicate like Japanese ramen. Oil noodles are yellow, white, or white spotted shiny noodles sold in plastic food bags in Chinese supermarkets. They can be thrown straight into the pan and stir fried. The shiny white Shanghai noodles are very pretty tossed together with green leeks and pink lobster (see Lobster with Ginger and Shanghai Noodles). Recently some famous brands have brought out 'stir fry noodles'. The Japanese udon varieties are the best.

Ramen are a soft Japanese egg noodle, best served in a hot chicken stock. Wun tun noodles are for Wun Tun Soup. Fensi (glass noodles), made from mung beans, are shiny and translucent. Soak them for 5 minutes in freshly boiled water until *al dente;* rinse. Served cold with shredded vegetables and a garlic dressing they make a wonderful summer noodle or spiced up with minced meat for a more substantial treat.

Rice stick noodles are well-known in the popular Singapore noodles, a stir fried assembly of leftover meat and vegetables in a curry paste. Fried with chicken breast and a savoury fish sauce they make a lovely light snack (see Vermicelli with Griddled Chicken), served hot or cold.

River noodles (*hofun*) are the queen of noodles – the softest and most beautiful, yet more substantial and tasty than any other when tossed into a savoury stir fry. Blanch them for a couple of seconds until they can be shaken apart with chopsticks.

Well, how long is a stick of noodle? In China a stick of noodle is as long as your life. That's why short noodles all come from Japan! The especially long ones are reserved for special birthdays when the happy septagenarian has to suck up the longest stick without breaking it. Sharing the noodle dish with much sucking and slapping of lips will allow you to share in the luck and longevity of your host.

Basic Stir Fried Noodles

This is the archetypal stir fried meal-in-one noodle dish which you can adapt to your taste, adding finely sliced leftover meats and shredded vegetables, so long as you are sensitive to their cooking times or lightly poach them beforehand.

Heat the wok and add 1 tablespoon of oil. When it is just smoking, turn the beansprouts in the oil for 1 minute, then remove and drain.

Add the remaining oil to the wok and reheat. Scatter in the pork and stir until the meat changes colour. Then throw in the noodles, salt, soy sauce, bean paste, sugar, pickle, stock and spring onions.

Stir and mix thoroughly for 4 minutes, then return the beansprouts to the wok with the sesame oil and wine. Stir fry for a further 2 minutes.

Serves 2

2 tbsp vegetable or peanut oil

210 g/7 oz beansprouts

150 g/5 oz lean pork, cut across the grain into matchsticks

240 g/8 oz/1 cup yellow oil noodles

½ tsp salt

½ tbsp dark soy sauce

1 tbsp hot bean paste or chilli sauce

1 tsp granulated sugar

30 g/1 oz shredded Sichuan pickle (*zha cai*), finely chopped

1½ tbsp enhanced stock (see page 147)

3 spring onions (scallions), finely chopped

1 tsp sesame oil

1 tbsp *Shaoxing* (rice) wine or medium sherry

Our Secret
Fresh oil noodles are easy to find in Chinese supermarkets and are increasingly available in the major supermarket chains. Many of the newly marketed, long-life 'straight to wok' noodles are rather hard and don't have the delicate flavour of the fresher versions. If you are using this kind remove the pork after the initial stir frying and cook the noodles a little longer in the sauce before returning the meat to the pan. Look for the Japanese brands of white wheat noodles (*udon*). Japanese noodle companies have a longer experience of serving large supermarket chains and produce softer, frozen noodles.

noodle dishes 89

Black Bean Beef and River Noodles (*Hofun*)

Serves 4

360 g/12 oz fresh *hofun* or 180 g/6 oz dried

400 g/14 oz lean beef, cut into thin 4 cm/1½ in strips

1½ tsp salt

1 egg white

1½ tbsp cornflour (cornstarch)

4 tbsp vegetable or peanut oil

1 Spanish onion, thinly sliced

2 slices fresh root ginger, finely sliced

2 cloves garlic, crushed and finely chopped

2 tbsp black beans, soaked in water for 3 minutes, drained and chopped

1 tbsp light soy sauce

1½ tbsp oyster sauce

1 tbsp hot bean paste or chilli sauce

4 tbsp stock

1 red (bell) pepper, cored, seeded and cut into thin strips

3 spring onions (scallions), cut into 3 cm/1¼ in sections

This is a standard Cantonese dish served in many Chinese restaurants in Britain. In this recipe we recommend using fresh hofun, which is softer and more elastic than the dried version.

Cook the *hofun* as per the packet instructions, then soak in cold water to prevent them sticking and drain until ready to use. Rub the beef with the salt, dip in egg white and dust with cornflour.

Heat the wok and then add the oil. When it just begins to smoke, scatter in the beef and stir fry quickly until the meat changes colour. Remove the beef with a slotted spoon and set aside. Drain off and reserve the oil and wipe the wok with kitchen paper (kitchen towels).

Reheat 2 tablespoons of oil in the wok. Add the onion and ginger and stir fry for 1 minute. Add the garlic, black beans, soy sauce, oyster sauce, bean paste and stock. Bring to the boil, then add the beef and red pepper, stirring constantly.

Add the *hofun* and spring onions. Turn up the heat as high as possible, turning together for 2 minutes. The hofun tends to stick together, so keep the mixture moving, but not too vigorously, as the *hofun* may break. If the mixture is too dry and keeps sticking, add a little more stock.

Our Secret

Oil left over from the initial deep-frying of meat and seafood is flavoured and can be used again. Strain it well and heat it again with a piece of fresh ginger. Keep a special sealed bottle, marked as flavoured oil. The more flavoured the oil, the tastier the stir fry.

Ants Climbing the Trees

Sichuan's answer to spaghetti Bolognese should be red with chilli, not tomatoes. But you can make it as hot or bland as you like. The ants themselves are the minced meat pieces crawling around the shiny translucent noodles!

Soak the mushrooms in hot water for 30 minutes, remove the hard stalks and finely slice the caps. Reserve the soaking water. Heat the oil, swirling it around the wok until it begins to smoke. Stir fry the meat until it browns.

Add the mushrooms, pepper, garlic, hot bean paste and wine, then stir fry for 2 minutes. Add the soy sauce, noodles, stock and mushroom water. Simmer for 5 minutes. Remove from the heat and sprinkle with Sichuan pepper. Stir and serve.

Serves 2

3 Chinese dried mushrooms

2 tbsp vegetable or peanut oil

120 g/4oz/½ cup minced pork or beef

½ green (bell) pepper, cored, seeded and finely chopped

2 cloves garlic, finely chopped

2 tbsp hot bean paste

2 tbsp *Shaoxing* (rice) wine or medium sherry

2 tbsp light soy sauce

120 g/4 oz *fensi* (glass noodles), soaked in boiling water until *al dente* (about 5 minutes)

250 ml/8 fl oz/1 cup chicken stock

1 tsp ground Sichuan pepper

Our Secret
For a family dish simply reduce the hot bean paste and double the quantities. This is truly a meal in minutes – good by itself or as a spicy slant to a banquet. You can also use lamb mince, but increase the proportion of garlic in the recipe.

Lobster with Ginger and Shanghai Noodles

Serves 6

2 x 750 g/1½ lb lobsters
(see Our Secret)

vegetable oil for
deep-frying

10 slices fresh root ginger,
shredded

4 large spring onions
(scallions) or 2 leeks, cut
in half lengthways and
then on the diagonal into
2.5 cm/1 in sections

1 tsp salt

1 kg/2¼ lb thick, white
Shanghai noodles

250 ml/8 fl oz/1 cup
enhanced stock (see
page 147)

3 tbsp dark soy sauce

4 tbsp *Shaoxing* (rice) wine
or medium sherry

This dish is most magnificent as a starter for a banquet, or simply by itself for a lighter meal. Splashes of pink lobster vibrate against the glossy white of the noodles. Be really Chinese and cover the table with piles of pink shells. You can also use fresh crab if you prefer.

Place the lobster on its back and chop through lengthways with one quick motion. Then divide it into large bite-size pieces.

Heat the wok and add the oil. When it just begins to smoke, add the lobster pieces and stir them around gently for 3 minutes. When the shell has turned pink, remove and pour off the oil.

Return 2 tablespoons of oil to the pan and stir fry the ginger, spring onions and salt for a minute. Add the noodles, stock, soy sauce and wine and bring it all to the boil over a high heat.

Return the lobster to the pan and mix everything together. Cover the pan and leave to cook over high heat for another 3–4 minutes, reducing the liquid until it has thickened to a sauce. Turn everything into a big serving bowl.

Our Secret
It's best to chop the lobster just before stir frying, preferably while it is chilled and slightly dozy, otherwise it is just too lively to cleave down the middle with one sharp chop. If you're squeamish get the fishmonger to do it in advance. But do so on the same day. Make sure you buy small lobsters because they are tastier.

Dan Dan Noodles

Dan dan noodles are so popular that there are many shops and stalls in Sichuan that sell only small bowls of this snack.

Mix the oils, soy sauce, stock, sesame paste and garlic and heat in the wok.

Add the beansprouts and stir and toss for a couple of minutes until heated through. Add the sesame oil, noodles and wine. Stir to coat well and turn out into two bowls.

Sprinkle each bowl with the chopped spring onions and ground peanuts.

Serves 2

½ tbsp chilli oil

1 tbsp vegetable
or peanut oil

2½ tbsp dark soy sauce

2 tbsp reduced stock
(beef stock is traditional)

2 tbsp sesame paste or
dark tahini

2 cloves garlic, crushed
and finely chopped

1 small handful
beansprouts

1 tbsp sesame oil

240 g/8 oz white Shanghai
or fresh noodles, blanched
briefly

1 tbsp *Shaoxing* (rice) wine
or medium sherry

2 spring onions (scallions),
finely chopped

2 tsp ground peanuts

Our Secret
If you use noodles that are boiled for only a few minutes the sauce and bean curd will cook in their heat – simply mix the sauce ingredients in each bowl while the noodles are cooking and then assemble at the last minute.

Vermicelli with Griddled Chicken

Serves 2–3

4 Chinese dried
mushrooms

240 g/8 oz rice stick
noodles

1½ chicken breasts, cut
into thin strips (shredded)

pinch of salt

½ egg white

vegetable oil for frying

For the dressing:

1 clove garlic, crushed and
finely chopped

¼ red chilli and ¼ green
chilli, seeded and finely
chopped

1 tbsp white wine vinegar

½ tsp fish sauce

2 tbsp enhanced stock
(see page 147)

1 tsp chilli oil or hot bean
paste

1 tsp dark soy sauce

pinch salt

juice of ¼ lemon

chopped coriander
(cilantro) or flat-leaf parsley
to garnish

Rice noodles tossed with golden chicken and a light lemon and chilli dressing make a delicate and delicious lunch or supper dish. This dish is equally good served hot or cold.

Soak the mushrooms in hot water for 30 minutes, remove the hard stalks and finely slice the caps. Soak the noodles in hot water for 10 minutes and rinse, or prepare according to packet instructions.

Sprinkle the chicken breast with salt and mix with the egg white. Marinate in the refrigerator for 30 minutes.

Lightly coat a griddle or cast-iron frying pan with vegetable oil. When hot scatter on the chicken and press lightly with a spatula to flatten the meat.

Griddle till the pieces begin to turn golden brown then turn and press down on the other side. When the chicken is almost cooked through, add the Chinese mushrooms and toss together.

Meanwhile bring a large pot of water to the boil. Add the noodles and bring back to the boil. Blanch for 10 seconds and drain thoroughly. Place the noodles on a warm plate and arrange the chicken and mushrooms on top.

Combine all the dressing ingredients and 1 tbsp of water together, then dress the chicken and noodles. Sprinkle with coriander (cilantro) or parsley to serve.

Our Secret

Tim Diep, our young Vietnamese chef, taught us this dish and it has become a favourite among our customers. You will have to adjust this recipe to the brand of rice stick noodles you are using. Some simply need to be soaked in boiling water, others require boiling as described above. The noodles should be firm but not hard. A trial run with a small handful only takes a few seconds.

Black Bean Seafood

This is the dish that father's dreams were made of and, after Singapore noodles, must be the most popular dish, favoured by our more discerning customers. The juxtaposition of the fresh-tasting seafood, the strong savouriness of the black bean and the substantial egg noodles gives a taste and texture full of vibrant contrast.

Halve the squid and score with criss-crossing lines on the inside, then cut into small 2 cm x 3 cm/¾ in x 1¼ in pieces. Heat the wok, then add the oil. When it just begins to smoke, stir fry the prawns and squid together for 30 seconds. Pour away all the excess oil.

Add the garlic, chilli and the black beans and turn together for a further 30 seconds. Add the onions, peppers and mussels, soy sauce, oyster sauce, sugar and noodles.

Mix thoroughly and stir fry for 3 minutes. Add the *Shaoxing* wine and sesame oil and turn together for 30 seconds. Serve immediately.

Serves 2

1 squid

oil for deep-frying

8 tiger prawns, shelled and deveined

3 cloves garlic, crushed

fresh chilli pepper

1 tbsp black beans, chopped roughly and soaked in hot water for 10 minutes

1 small Spanish onion, sliced

½ red (bell) pepper, finely sliced

½ green (bell) pepper, finely sliced

15 small cooked mussels

1 tbsp dark soy sauce

2 tbsp oyster sauce

1 tsp granulated sugar

500 g/1 lb yellow oil noodles

2 tbsp *Shaoxing* (rice) wine or medium sherry

2 tsp sesame oil

Our Secret

At the height of lunch time business in our restaurant The Teahouse we will have multiple orders for the same dish. Two portions in the wok are ideal if you have a decent flame on your cooker. On a jet-fired turbo flame you can stir fry up to three portions in a large wok at any one time. If the fluids dry quickly the noodles will char and burn – no bad thing if you like the taste of barbecues, but it is easy to overdo it, so be careful.

Glass Noodles with Chinese Cabbage

Serves 4 with a casseroled dish and other vegetable, or as one among many banquet dishes to go with rice

For the sauce:

2 tbsp light soy sauce

3 tbsp chicken stock

2 tsp chilli sauce

1 tbsp white wine vinegar

1½ tbsp *Shaoxing* (rice) wine or medium sherry

1 tbsp sesame paste

For the noodles:

4 tbsp vegetable oil

360 g/12 oz/1½ cups Chinese cabbage, cut into 1 cm/½ in slices

3 celery stalks, cut into strips 5 mm x 2.5 cm/¼ in x 1 in

1 clove garlic, crushed

2 spring onions (scallions), cut lengthways, then into 5 cm/2 in sections

2 small red chillies, seeded and cut into fine slices

1½ tsp salt and pepper to taste

120 g/4 oz fensi (glass noodles), soaked in hot water for 5 minutes

coriander (cilantro) to garnish

This is a simple light-coloured dish, quick to prepare and subtly flavoured, that can be used as the staple with other stronger-flavoured dishes. It is basically nutty and savoury but has a touch of chilli hot and vinegar sour.

Combine the sauce ingredients.

Heat the wok and add the oil. When just smoking, add the Chinese cabbage, celery, garlic, spring onions and chilli and sprinkle with salt and pepper. Toss and turn for 1½ minutes over a high heat, then add the noodles.

When you have mixed the noodles and vegetables and heated them through pour in the sauce. Stir fry together over a medium heat for two minutes. Then cover and leave to simmer over a low heat for 2 more minutes. Garnish with coriander (cilantro) to serve.

Our Secrets

Kept chilled, Chinese cabbage will stay fresh and crunchy for weeks and can be lightly stir fried, served raw as salad, or added to a clear stock with noodles (especially fensi). Raw, it is sweet and juicy, and when stir fried it retains its freshness.

I will never forget one day at the start of winter collecting my daughter from her nursery in the North-Eastern suburb of Beijing. The playground swimming pool, from the shallow end to the deep end, was immersed in literally thousands of the light green and white heads of Chinese cabbage.

Zhajiang Noodles

Yet another refreshing alternative to Bolognese for a family meal, this is especially fun for tossing all the ingredients together at the table. The brilliance of the carrots and mangetout stand out against the shining white noodles and the ruddy brown sauce.

Divide the cucumber, carrot, beansprouts, mangetout and spring onions by the number of diners and lay out in a heap on the side of each plate.

Heat the wok and add the oil. When it just starts to smoke, add the onion and ginger and fry for 1 minute, then add the meat and chopped garlic. Stir fry together for 3 minutes then reduce the heat.

Add the yellow bean paste, soy sauce and sugar. Stir fry on a high heat for a further 3 minutes, keeping the food moving constantly to avoid sticking. Then add the stock and cook for a further 3 minutes. Finally add the sesame oil and wine and turn the whole dish together for another 10 seconds.

Meanwhile, blanch the noodles until they are heated through and place next to the vegetables. (If you are using dried egg noodles cook them according to instructions, but remove from the heat just before they are cooked. Drain and rinse thoroughly under cold water.) Pour the sauce on the other side of the noodles. Each diner tosses together their own meal.

Serves 3–4

10 cm/4 in section cucumber, cut into long, thin strips

1 carrot, peeled and shredded

handful each of beansprouts and mangetout, blanched for a second, drained and left to dry

4 spring onions (scallions), chopped into 6 cm/2½ in sections and sliced lengthways

2 tbsp vegetable or peanut oil

1 medium onion, finely chopped

2 slices fresh root ginger, finely chopped

300 g/10 oz minced pork

2 cloves garlic, crushed

1 tbsp yellow bean paste

1 tbsp dark soy sauce

2 tsp white granulated sugar

4 tbsp chicken stock

½ tsp sesame oil

½ tbsp *Shaoxing* (rice) wine or medium sherry

500 g/1 lb/2 cups fresh white Shanghai noodles

Our Secrets

Everyone has their own version of Zhajiang Noodles, this favourite lunchtime snack. At its simplest you just need carrots and cucumber and if you can find the elusive product, sweet bean sauce, this will do on its own.

Oil noodles live up to their name so it is important not to add too much extra fat. Otherwise the dish is very flexible and you can add and subtract vegetables that cook quickly and are to your taste.

Glass Noodles with Spinach and Beansprouts

Serves 4 with another dish

4 Chinese dried
mushrooms

1½ tbsp dried shrimps
(optional)

120 g/4 oz fensi (glass
noodles), soaked in boiling
water until *al dente*
(about 5 minutes)

2 tbsp dark soy sauce

1 tbsp light soy sauce

1½ tsp white wine vinegar

4 tbsp vegetable or
peanut oil

2 cloves garlic, finely
chopped

2 slices fresh root ginger,
finely chopped

240 g/8 oz young spinach

240 g/8 oz beansprouts

This is an attractive, nourishing dish with a complex array of flavours to tantalise the palate. Preparation is almost too simple. Serve in individual bowls with a cold sliced meat, another vegetable or salad for a light lunch. For a larger banquet it can be one of a number of other dishes to go with rice.

Soak the mushrooms for 30 minutes in hot water, remove any hard stalks and slice the caps, then return the mushrooms to the soaking water. Soak the shrimps, if using, in hot water for 30 minutes, roughly chop and return to the soaking water. Drain and cut the noodles to 13 cm/5 in lengths with a pair of scissors.

Add the noodles to a bowl containing the mushrooms and dried shrimps. Add the soy sauces and vinegar. Turn and mix the contents well together, so that the noodles can absorb the flavour and liquid.

Heat the wok and add the oil. When hot, but before the oil begins to smoke turn the garlic and ginger once in the oil. Then immediately throw in the spinach and bean sprouts, and toss to coat them in the oil. Keep stirring and turning for 1 minute.

Our Secret
Lili Xiong, a friend and adviser on vegetarian food, first tutored me in the secrets of preparing making fensi. As they are made from powdered mung beans they are almost treated like a vegetable and not a noodle and their shiny, translucence often enhances soup, stir fried or casseroled dishes. Very frequently they are used to supplement dumpling and wrapper fillings, especially in vegetarian dim sum where not only are they a source of protein, but they also absorb the flavours of sauces.

Add the noodles with the shrimps and mushrooms and any liquid in the bowl. Add the wine, stock and butter. Sprinkle with salt and sugar and half the spring onions or all of the *jiu cai*. Slowly toss all the ingredients together while they are heating up. Allow the contents to come to the boil, reduce heat to low and simmer gently for 4 minutes.

Sprinkle the contents of the wok with sesame oil, the remaining spring onions and pepper. Give a final big stir and turn out into a large serving bowl. Garnish with coriander (cilantro) or watercress.

3 tbsp *Shaoxing* (rice) wine or medium sherry

3–4 tbsp chicken stock

60 g/2 oz/½ stick butter

2 tsp salt

2 tsp granulated white sugar

4 *jiu cai* (Chinese chives), cut into 2.5 cm/1 in sections, or spring onions (scallions), cut in half lengthways then into 2.5 cm/1 in sections

2 tbsp sesame oil

¼ tsp freshly ground pepper

coriander (cilantro) or watercress to garnish (optional)

Beef or Chinese River Noodles (*Hofun*)

Serves 2

500 g/1 lb/2 cups fresh
hofun, or 240g/8 oz dried

300 g/10 oz lean
beef or chicken, thinly
sliced and cut into
5 cm/2 in squares

½ tsp salt

pinch of pepper

4 tbsp vegetable or
peanut oil

½ tbsp fresh root ginger,
finely chopped

½ small green (bell)
pepper, cored, seeded
and finely sliced

½ small red (bell) pepper,
cored, seeded and finely
sliced

½ medium Spanish onion,
finely sliced

1 tsp hot bean paste or
chilli sauce

½ tbsp dark soy sauce

½ tbsp light soy sauce

1 tbsp oyster sauce

½ tbsp sesame oil

1 tbsp *Shaoxing* (rice) wine
or medium sherry

sesame seeds, lightly
toasted

Hofun *are the queen of all noodles – these thick flat streamers are so soft, moist and brilliantly white that they literally gleam when dressed in this oyster-sauce based coating with the green and red peppers.*

Prepare the *hofun* as per the packet instructions, then soak in cold water to prevent sticking. Rub the beef or chicken with the salt, pepper and ½ teaspoon of oil. Break the fresh *hofun* up into strands.

Heat the remaining oil in a wok over a high heat until it just begins to smoke. Stir fry the beef or chicken for 10 seconds and then turn down the heat, still turning in the oil, until all the pieces have changed colour. Immediately pour away as much of the oil as possible. Set the beef or chicken aside in a warm place.

Add the ginger, the vegetables, the hot bean paste, soy and oyster sauces and the fresh or par-cooked noodles to the pan. Turn up the heat as high as possible, turning together for 1 minute (longer if you are using fresh noodles). The *hofun* will tend to stick together and to the pan. Beat them gently with the back of the wok ladle and keep them moving, although not too vigorously or they may break. If the mixture is too dry and keeps sticking, add a little more oil.

Return the meat or chicken to the pan, add the sesame oil and wine and stir for a further 1 minute. Turn out on to a dish and sprinkle with toasted sesame seeds to serve.

Our Secrets

Hofun may require careful handling, since they suddenly turn from being hard and stuck together to being very soft and easy to break up. The best way is to wet your hands and gently separate the strands before cooking. If they are separated in advance the cooking time is lessened which keeps the noodles a brilliant white and prevents them becoming infused with the brown colour of the sauce.

It is worth taking the time to learn how to serve this dish, so that you can adapt the recipe to all the meats and vegetables that you like.

Hot Salad Noodles

The carrot, pepper, mangetout, water chestnuts and bamboo shoots add up to an amazing array of crunchy textures. Combined with the fleshy mushrooms and wood ear as well as the savoury noodles, this dish is a real treat.

If using, soak the wood ear in warm water overnight, drain and cut into strips. Soak the mushrooms in hot water for 30 minutes, remove the hard stalks and finely slice the caps. Heat the wok and add the oil. When it just begins to smoke add the garlic, ginger and mushroom and wood ear and turn in the oil for a few seconds.

Then add all of the vegetables and turn in the oil for 30 seconds. Add the stock, salt, pepper, sugar, light soy sauce, vegetarian oyster sauce and the noodles and stir fry together for 2 minutes.

Finally add the sesame oil and *Shaoxing* wine. Turn together for a further 30 seconds and serve.

Serves 2

45 g/1½ oz wood ear (optional)

3 Chinese dried mushrooms

1 tbsp vegetable or peanut oil

2 cloves garlic, crushed

1 cm/½ in piece fresh root ginger, finely chopped

60 g/2 oz carrot, finely sliced on the diagonal

½ medium Spanish onion, sliced

60 g/2 oz mangetout

60 g/2 oz each red and green (bell) pepper, cored, seeded and thinly sliced

handful of beansprouts

30 g/1 oz bamboo shoots

30 g/1 oz sliced water chestnuts

2 tbsp enhanced vegetable or chicken stock (see page 145 or 146)

pinch each of salt, pepper and sugar

½ tbsp light soy sauce

½ tbsp vegetarian oyster sauce

500 g/1 lb/2 cups yellow oil noodles

½ tbsp sesame oil

½ tbsp *Shaoxing* (rice) wine or medium sherry

Our Secret
Whenever you see a recipe with such a long list of ingredients and think it's just a bit of this and a bit of that, you are probably right! Some of the best Chinese food comes from leftovers – and in China necessity is definitely the mother of invention. Here you can adapt the recipe to whatever vegetables you have. It is simply necessary to mimic the spirit of the dish which is to combine crunchy and savouriness, by choosing the vegetables carefully and cooking them quickly in a very savoury sauce.

Rice and Breads

On the secret virtue of staples

For centuries, rice and the rice bowl has been a metaphor for material life, your livelihood and morality. You must always eat up the rice in your bowl. And should you ever drop a grain of rice, you had better pray for the starving millions, because you might just join them in your next life. Washing the rice until the water runs clear is a kind of ritual way of beginning the main stir frying and final preparation of the dishes. The meal is only 20 minutes away and the cleansing of the rice seems to clarify the chef's thoughts as well as remove impurities from the grain.

In this chapter we give recipies for the best way to cook the most common forms of rice available. Most Chinese cooks use American long grain or basmati rice, although a shorter slightly stickier rice holds together well and is easier to pick up with chopsticks. Thai fragrant rice is really the best for this purpose, but it's also the most expensive. In the end it's really a matter of personal taste.

Yesterday's rice is boiled into *xifan* (a kind of rice porridge or *congee* for short), a breakfast speciality served with savoury meats and pickled vegetables. Perfect light and smooth *congee* is made from a combination of glutinous and long-grain rice boiled in stock to make it savoury. A beef stock will make a very substantial meal; a lighter vegetable stock will make a staple to accompany dishes of a stronger flavour.

Congee is a treat for the digestion, especially for the young, the old, the diet conscious and the convalescent, and when made with fish or mushrooms it has a delicate flavour.

Another way of using yesterday's rice is to fry it up with chopped meat, seafood, eggs and vegetables (See Home-style Fried Rice). Hot fresh rice is no good because it allows the oil to penetrate and mushes too easily. When re-fried, yesterday's slightly dry grains separate and make a light, non-greasy meal in one.

In Northern China, wheat, in the form of flour and noodles, still just takes precedence over rice – with the ubiquitous mantou a clear favourite. We have also included a number of Northern breads and pancakes that probably originate in the Moslem community: *laobing*, a cross between chapati and naan bread, but with exquisite soft, feathery layers inside, are designed to accompany curries and meat or vegetable casseroles. And we are particularly grateful to Zhou Xun and her mother who provided the recipe for Bread Fish, a snack from their hometown Chengdu, capital of Sichuan.

Perfect Rice

Chinese almost always use the absorption method to cook rice, although there are a few different methods. The most critical issue is in the ratio of rice to water: a close standard of two parts rice to three parts water changes according to the amounts used. So with lesser amounts of rice you need proportionately more water and with greater amounts, less. This is probably because with lesser amounts a greater proportion of the surface water is directly exposed to heat and it therefore evaporates quickly. Ideally the rice should be soft and, not like risotto rice, al dente. For ease of eating with chopsticks it should cluster without being mushy. Short-grain rice needs less water because it is starchier: Thai fragrant rice therefore uses less water than ordinary long-grain. Here is our way of cooking long-grain rice using the absorption method in five simple stages:

1   Wash the rice until the rinsing water runs clear. This will separate the grains when they cook.

2   Add the water and a dash of oil to prevent sticking.

3   Bring to the boil.

4   Cover and reduce to a slow simmer for 10 minutes.

5   Leave, covered, for another 10 minutes or up to 30 minutes before serving.

Do not remove the cover of the saucepan while it is cooking. This may be a ritual prohibition, but it also keeps the moisture in the pan.

Our Secret
Father taught an apparently foolproof method of cooking ordinary long-grain rices or basmati. Just stick your finger into the rice, and bring the water about 1 cm/¾ in above it. Increase or decrease slightly according to the amounts that you use.

Home-styled Fried Rice

Serves 4

150 ml/5fl oz/⅔ cup
vegetable or peanut oil

120 g/4 oz young leeks,
finely chopped

6 eggs, beaten

500 g/1 lb/2 cups cooked
prawns (shrimp)

120 g/4 oz frozen peas,
blanched and drained

120 g/4 oz canned
sweetcorn (optional)

750 g/1½ lb leftover
cooled, cooked long-grain
rice, grains gently
separated with wet hands

Fried rice is a snack or light lunch and not part of a regular meal. Our recipe probably reflects traditions from the South-Eastern province of Fuzhou where eggs and seafood are added to the rice. No doubt the frozen peas were Father's addition. We would eat this at any time and it is a particular favourite with young children who like the sweet touch of canned sweetcorn.

Heat the wok and add the oil. When it just begins to smoke, stir fry the leeks for 30 seconds or until just soft. Push to the side of the pan. Pour in the beaten egg and leave until it begins to form an omelette. Then gently stir it until it all hardens.

Add the prawns (shrimp), peas and sweetcorn, if using, and mix everything together gently so that the egg breaks up into chunky pieces and heats through.

Add the rice. If it is lumpy, beat it against the side of the pan with the back of a spoon, taking care not to smash the other ingredients. Stir all the ingredients together and heat through. Serve hot.

Our Secrets

Fried rice is most representative of the frugality of Chinese culinary tradition – the ability to make tasty every last little bit of leftover food. For fried rice, it is essential to use yesterday's long-grain rice. Fresh rice is too soft and doesn't separate well when fried.

The most famous fried rice is said to come from Yangzhou, where shrimps, ham, chicken, peas, beansprouts and spring onions (scallions) are used. Cantonese chefs might add soy sauce and sliced roast pork, and often sprinkle in stock powder at the last minute, but if you have fresh ingredients the dish is tasty without.

Steamed Lotus Leaf Rice

This is our version of a famous dish served at special occasions, but which can also be found sold on the street wrapped in bamboo leaves and stuffed with all manner of sweet and savoury delights. Serve this as a snack or instead of rice at dinner. Brought to the table in a bamboo steamer the lotus leaf parcels bring the thrill of unwrapping presents to your party.

Soak the mushrooms in hot water for 30 minutes, remove the hard stalks and quarter the caps. Reserve the soaking water. Place the rice in an oiled heatproof dish and sprinkle with salt and 1 tablespoon of oil. Pour on 450 ml/15 fl oz/scant 2 cups water.

Place the dish in a steamer and steam for 30 minutes. Divide into four piles. Meanwhile, marinate the chicken for 20 minutes in the sugar, soy sauce, ground ginger, five-spice and sesame oil.

Heat the wok and add the remaining oil. When it just begins to smoke, scatter in the chicken and mushroom pieces and turn in the oil. Add the marinade, wine and the mushroom soaking water and bring to the boil. Turn down the heat and simmer for about 8 minutes. Add the wind-dried sausage and bring back to the boil, simmering for a further couple of minutes.

Meanwhile divide the rice into 4 portions, divide each portion of rice in half and shape into a large flat square in the middle of each half of a lotus leaf. Take a quarter of the chicken and sausage mixture and spoon it into the centre of the rice. Take the other half portion of rice. Shape into a flat square and cover the stuffing, working it together at the sides to seal it in. Then fold the leaves like a parcel around the rice. Repeat for the other leaves. Steam vigorously for 30 minutes.

Serves 4

8 Chinese dried mushrooms

500 g/1 lb glutinous rice, rinsed well

pinch of salt

2 tbsp vegetable or peanut oil

240 g/8 oz chicken breast, cut roughly into 1 cm/½ in cubes

1 tbsp *Shaoxing* (rice) wine or medium sherry

60 g/2 oz Chinese wind-dried sausage or thin Italian salami, chopped into 1 cm/½ in pieces (optional)

For the marinade:

pinch of sugar

2 tbsp dark soy sauce

2 tsp ground ginger

1 tsp five-spice powder

1 tbsp sesame oil

2 large lotus leaves, soaked in hot water for 10 minutes and halved

Our Secrets

The halved lotus leaves are big enough to wrap the rice parcels easily. If you place them fold side down in the steamer they won't unravel and are easy to unwrap at the table.

For a festive sweet variation, try filling the rice with red bean paste or red date paste.

Fish Congee

Serves 8

10 Chinese dried mushrooms

240 g/8 oz long-grain rice (or 120 g/4 oz glutinous rice and 120 g/4 oz long-grain)

3 litres/5 pints/12½ cups reduced chicken or fish stock

3 tbsp vegetable or peanut oil

1 onion, finely sliced

3 tbsp Sichuan pickle (*zha cai*), finely shredded

1 cm/½ in piece fresh root ginger, very thinly sliced

2 tbsp dark soy sauce

1 tbsp sesame oil

240 g/8 oz cod or haddock fillet, thinly sliced lengthways

240 g/8 oz cooked prawns (shrimp)

lettuce and coriander (cilantro) leaves, to serve

This is a warm soup-like rice dish which is very good when you want something simple. It's also perfect for the diet conscious, the convalescent and anyone feeling feeble. If you are unused to eating porridge-like savoury dishes you may find the consistency of congee a bit gooey, but this is a good chance to reform your sensibilities.

Soak the mushrooms in hot water for 30 minutes, remove the hard stalks and finely slice the caps. Reserve the soaking water.

Rinse the rice thoroughly and put it in a heavy casserole with the stock. Bring to the boil. Turn down the heat to medium and boil for 5 minutes. Stir well and cover. Turn to the lowest heat possible and simmer for about 1 hour, adding water if the rice begins to stick to the pan. The final consistency should be like porridge.

Heat the oil in a wok until it begins to smoke, then add the onion and toss for 30 seconds. Add the mushrooms, pickle and ginger and stir for about 1 minute. Mix in the soy sauce and mushroom soaking water. Bring to the boil, then reduce the heat and simmer until the mushrooms have absorbed most of the liquid. Finally turn up the heat and mix in the sesame oil.

When the rice is ready, add the fish, prawns (shrimp) and mushroom mixture to the casserole and mix together. Stir gently until the fish is cooked. Serve with lettuce and coriander (cilantro) leaves.

Our Secret

Xifan or *congee* is best made from glutinous rice, but it is most commonly made with yesterday's plain rice or a combination of both. It is a standard breakfast dish eaten together with pickles, eggs or cold meats and before sweet or savoury breakfast buns and cakes.

Mushroom *Congee*

This is our family's answer to risotto, a hearty dish for winter and autumn. We have made the consistency drier than usual to make it more acceptable to the Western palate.

Soak the dried mushrooms in hot water for 30 minutes, remove the hard stalks, quarter the caps and reserve the soaking water.

Place the rice in a heavy casserole with the stock. Bring to the boil, reduce the heat to medium and boil for 5 minutes. Stir well and cover. Reduce to the lowest heat possible and simmer for about 1 hour, adding water if the rice begins to stick. The final consistency should be sticky, but thicker than porridge.

Heat the oil until it begins to smoke, then add the onion. Toss to coat with oil for 30 seconds. Add all the mushrooms and the pickle and stir fry rapidly for about 2 minutes. Mix in the soy sauce, reserved mushroom soaking water, sugar and salt to taste.

Bring to the boil, then reduce the heat and simmer until the mushrooms have absorbed most of the liquid. Turn up the heat and mix in the sesame oil. Pour the contents of the wok into the casserole with the rice and mix well.

Serves 4

10 Chinese dried mushrooms

240 g/8 oz long-grain rice, rinsed

2 litres/3½ pints/8 cups stock (see Our Secrets)

5 tbsp vegetable or peanut oil

1 onion, sliced

210 g/7 oz button mushrooms, sliced

half an 8 oz can straw mushrooms, drained

1 tbsp Sichuan pickle (*zha cai*), finely shredded

2 tbsp dark soy sauce

1 tbsp crushed rock sugar, or granulated sugar

salt to taste

1 tbsp sesame oil

Our Secrets

Beef stock will make the *congee* very substantial, while a vegetable stock will lighten it a little.

Served with salad or French (green) beans, and made into vegetable stock this dish can be eaten as a vegetarian main course. Alternatively, serve it as an accompaniment to meat.

Millet *Congee* with Peanuts and Red Dates

Serves 4

360 g/12 oz millet, washed
thoroughly

30 red dates

60 g/2 oz peanuts, boiled
for 10 minutes

For congee the best millet comes from Qinzhou according to a connoisseur. Congee is a matter for culinary snobbery and there are restaurants whose menus are wholly devoted to serving as many different kinds as they can dream up. Like English pudding grains a small bowl of millet congee is lovely served with a sweet biscuit or cake. It is also good for fragile tummies and for those on a gluten-free diet (those with peanut allergies can substitute walnuts).

Boil 1.75 litres/3 pints/7½ cups water, then add the millet. Bring back to the boil and turn down to a slow simmer. Skim the scum from the surface of the water, then add the red dates. After 30 minutes, add the peanuts. Simmer for a further 30 minutes.

Our Secret
When plain boiled into a porridge or *congee*, millet has a naturally sweet, nutty flavour and is therefore preferable to other grains. Both peanut and red date impart their own different sweetness to the grain and so it is not necessary to add sugar or honey. Of course you can adjust the flavour to your taste. Scots will favour salt, while English will recall semolina and rice pudding and wish to add honey. Either is acceptable in China.

Spring Onion (Scallion) Pancakes

Spring onion (scallion) cakes go with any family meal and perfectly complement soup and vegetable dishes. We have also been served them in a Taiwanese restaurant with puff pastry: simply take a 30 cm/12 in sheet of pastry and begin by sprinkling it with spring onion and salt. Use less oil, but more spring onions since the pastry will puff up. Prepare as below, finishing by baking them in a very hot oven for 10 minutes. These must be eaten immediately.

Sieve the flours together into a bowl. Pour in 400 ml/14 fl oz/1⅔ cups boiling water in a thin stream, mixing thoroughly. Set aside for a few minutes before adding a few tablespoons of cold water to mix into a pliable dough. Cover with clingfilm and leave for 30 minutes.

Divide the dough into five pieces and roll out into a 30 cm/12 in pancake. Sprinkle with an even layer of spring onion and half a teaspoon of salt. Drizzle 1 tablespoon of oil evenly over the top and then roll the pancake into a long sausage.

Divide the sausage into four equal segments and pat and squeeze each one into a round. Flatten with the palm of the hand and roll out into a 10 cm/4 in pancake. You can experiment with the thickness of the pancakes – the thicker the pancakes are the softer they will be in the centre. On the other hand the addition of self-raising (self-rising) flour as well as rolling the pancakes very thin makes them crisp and avoids a stodgy centre.

Shallow-fry or griddle each pancake on each side in a little oil until browned, pressing down with a fish slice (spatula) so the whole surface browns. This should take 5 minutes.

Makes 20

400 g/14 oz/3½ cups plain (all-purpose) flour

120 g/4 oz/1 cup self-raising (self-rising) flour

10 tbsp finely chopped spring onions (only use the green part)

2½ tsp salt

150 ml/5 fl oz/⅔ cups vegetable oil

Our Secrets

If you don't want to cook 20 cakes at once the dough can be kept wrapped in the refrigerator for up to 48 hours. Vary the oil according to taste. Less oil will make the pancake like a chapati; children often prefer more.

The most moreish Spring Onion Pancakes we have tasted came from a breakfast vendor on the streets of Shanghai who had deep-fried them until puffy and golden brown.

Laobing

Makes 4 small pancakes

750 g/1½ lb plain
(all-purpose) flour

4 tsp salt to taste

3 tbsp sesame oil and
3 tbsp sesame paste or
dark tahini, mixed together

This is rather like an Indian chapati, except more sophisticated.

Sieve the flour and 2 teaspoons of salt into a bowl. Slowly pour in 250ml/8fl oz/1 cup cold water, mixing with a chopstick until the dough becomes firm, not sticky. Very lightly and quickly knead in the crumbs. Do not overwork or it will be very rubbery. Then cover the dough with a damp cloth and leave for 2–3 hours. Heat a heavy, flat-bottomed frying pan (skillet) over a very low heat for 20 minutes.

Lightly flour a work surface. Squeeze the dough into an long oblong shape. Cut into four sections and cover three with a damp cloth. Roll out with a section sat a time with a floured rolling pin. Keep turning the dough clockwise and work into a very thin, but still firm, rectangle (17 in x 9 in) using short even strokes. The larger the rectangle the more leaves there will be in the final pancake. Try not to stretch the dough and keep plenty of flour underneath it. Smear itall over with 1½ tablespoons of the sesame oil and paste. Sprinkle with salt.

Stretch out one end and fold down the corners. From that end, roll up the dough into a long sausage. Press down with the heel of your hand all along the seam. Bring each to the centre and press down.

Now, take the rolling pin and roll the dough into a round. Simultaneously pull the dough towards you and roll in the opposite direction, working in circular movements. The resulting pancake should be about 5 mm/¼ in thick and 20 cm/8 in in diameter. Repeat the process with the other three sections, keeping the completed *laobing* covered with a damp cloth. Do not stack them.

To cook, put a metal ring under the pan so that the heat distributes evenly. Keep shaking the pan to prevent sticking and uneven cooking. When the pancake bubbles and browns in patches all over the underside, flip it over and cook the other side (about 4 minutes

Our Secret
When it is made well the inside opens into soft, feathery layers of savoury pancake. That's the test. lit is quite easy to make an acceptable version, but with experience the leaves get finer and more numerous. Laobing should be eaten with a dish that has a lot of gravy or sauce.

Chinese Pancakes

These are the classic steamed pancakes served with Peking duck.
Serve them with Yellow Cassia Roll, Lamb in Cumin Sesame Cream
Sauce, Crispy Lamb Wrapped in Lettuce or Crispy Duck. It is easier to
buy them, but it is certainly less satisfying. This recipe is quite fun to
do. Just make sure you start an hour or so before ahead because
they have to stand for a while – or prepare them in advance.

Sieve the flour and sugar together, then mix in about 300 ml/10 fl oz/
1¼ cups warm water (more or less depending on the quality of the
flour) slowly with chopsticks until you have a crumbly dough. Press
together and knead gently for a couple of minutes. Cover and leave
for 30 minutes.

Knead the dough for a further 4 minutes. Divide it in half and then roll
into two long sausages, making sure that there are no fissures at the
two ends. Cut each sausage into 15 rounds.

Place one round on the heel of your palm and press the heel of your
other palm down on it firmly, flattening the dough. Then smear one
edge with sesame oil. Make another flat round and then press them
together to make a two-layered pancake. Now, if you are right
handed, slightly raise one edge of the double pancake and, holding
a small rolling pin with your right hand, simultaneously roll from the
centre of the pancake away from your body and gently pull and
shape the pancake into a 15 cm/6 in round with the left hand.

Gently heat a heavy, flat pan and dry-fry the pancake until it begins to
puff up and the underside begins to brown. Turn and cook the other
side (about 15 seconds per side). Remove and peel apart the two
pancakes. Fold each one in half with the cooked side on the inside.

When you are ready, steam the pancakes for about 5 minutes.

Makes 30

500 g/1 lb plain
(all-purpose) flour

1½ tsp white granulated
sugar

sesame oil for basting

Our Secret

It's a good thing to make extra pancakes. Unused pancakes that
have already been dry-fried can be wrapped in clingfilm (plastic
wrap) and frozen. To reconstitute simply re-steam for 10 minutes.

Bread Fish

Makes 12

240 g/8 oz Chinese chives
(*jiu cai*) (See Our Secret)

500 g/1 lb flour

2 heaped tsp salt

1 tsp freshly ground
Sichuan pepper

olive oil for deep-frying

This recipe comes from Xinfan, a small town outside Chengdu, the provincial capital of Sichuan, courtesy of the Zhou family who have turned bread into fish!

Wash the chives and cut finely. Put the flour into a bowl and mix with 400 ml/14 fl oz/1⅔ cups water, salt and Sichuan pepper and the chives. Beat with a wooden spoon until the mixture does not stick to the bowl. Roll out on a floured surface into a sheet 5 mm/¼ in thick and cut out 12 fish shapes.

Heat the oil in a wok until it begins to smoke. Add the fish one by one. Fry until they are golden brown and remove with a slotted spoon. Soak up any excess oil on kitchen paper (paper towels).

Serve as a snack or side dish on a bed of mixed green salad to complete the seascape!

Our Secret
Chinese chives, *jiu cai*, are only available seasonally, but we have found that an equal mixture of English chives, coriander (cilantro) and spring onion makes a delicious alternative. Using olive oil is also not authentic, but a delicious variation. Definitely a recipe to make with children.

Lamb Patties

You can make excellent patties with Laobing – here is one of our favourite recipes.

Combine the marinade ingredients, add the lamb and marinate for 1 hour.

Roll the dough into a long oblong shape, approximately 13 cm x 40 cm/5 in x 16 in (the longer it is the more layers you will have in the pastry).

Smear generously with the oil, paste and sprinkle with salt. Fold in the corners at the left end. Roll up the oblong from left to right and seal the seam. Fold over the two ends to meet in the middle, turn the dough over. Now roll out the dough again, but this time into a square shape. Divide into four equal squares.

Heat a very heavy bottomed cast-iron pan suitable for frying, a very low, slow heat is necessary. Press one quarter of the meat on one triangular half of the pastry, leaving a ½ in space around the edges. Wet the edges and gently press the sides together. Make up all four.

Cook as for the Laobing recipe.

Serves 4

For the marinade:

1 tbsp dark soy sauce

2 tbsp *Shaoxing* (rice) wine or medium sherry

pinch of salt

3 cloves garlic, crushed and finely chopped

4 slices fresh root ginger, finely chopped

pinch of pepper

1 tsp ground cumin

240 g/8 oz/1 cup minced lamb

dough for 1 laobing (see page 112), prepared as far as squeezing it into an oblong

1 tbsp vegetable or peanut oil AND SESAME PASTE??

Our Secret
The best way to cook these patties is without much evidence of heat or browning. The slower and deeper the heat the more satisfactory they are.

Pastes and Sauces

Chinese cooking made easy

A characteristic of Chinese cuisine is that all classic sauces are mixed freshly at the time of cooking. So, an inevitable trademark of the busy Chinese kitchen that there will always be oil, various soy sauces, sesame oil, salt, sugar, *Shaoxing* rice wine, vinegar, chilli sauce, perhaps fish sauce and other well known condiments.

The latter are mostly prepared from fermented soy products and soy sauce in particular. Soy sauce is made from the *da dou* (the big bean), a fermented mixture of boiled soy beans, wheat flour, salt brine and different fungi. There are many variations from high to low salt and rich to medium: light soy sauce is surprisingly much saltier and stronger than dark soy sauce which is used primarily for its colour. Mushroom soy sauce is a dark soy with extra flavour. With so many soy products, in the past, free salt was rarely used.

Reddish brown *hoisin* (sea fresh) sauce, is made from soy beans, flour, sugar, salt, garlic, vinegar, chilli, sesame oil and pepper, a combination which is simultaneously sweet and savoury with a tangy zing. Then there is the tremendously salty yellow beans or yellow bean paste, made from fermented soy beans flour and salt; *douban jiang* (hot bean paste) a mixture of the latter with added chilli from Sichuan, is an essential stir fry ingredient to keep by the cooker; black beans are another fermented soy bean, interrupted in their fermentation by roasting and blackening at a high temperature.

From Canton and the South comes oyster sauce, a surprisingly meaty flavoured sweet caramel sauce made from ground oysters, that makes a wonderful addition to stir fried red meats and some vegetables. There are also some very good vegetarian versions of oyster sauce.

Sweet and sour sauce originates in North-Eastern cuisine and was mainly served with yellow croaker fish and not ladled on to deep-fried chicken or pork as we so often find it in the West. The dish has been so thoroughly re-created (it did not originally include fruit) that it is almost not worth discussing in a Chinese cookbook. But, with respect to a judicious blend of tradition with innovation, we have included a hybrid version to go with fish that is at least as sour and hot as it is sweet (see Sea Bass with Sweet and Sour Hot Bean Sauce)!

Note that for all these sauces a quantity is not given. The idea is to make a batch and to use as and when needed.

Wine Sediment Paste

Ever since editing Father's autobiography, wine sediment paste has been one of those deliciously unsolved mysteries – it was one of his ongoing culinary fantasies to re-create from memory of his childhood in Fuzhou. Here is our fake recipe, adapted from one of Father's more imaginative flourishes. It is a rich, hot alcoholic paste suitable for stir frying, braising and smearing on poultry before roasting.

Put all the ingredients except the brandy into a liquidiser and process until smooth. Heat and stir the mixture together in a heavy-based pan, preferably a proper copper sauce-making pan. Simmer until it is reduced by at least a half to a thick paste. Stir in the brandy and set aside. The sauce will keep in a covered jar for at least a week in the refrigerator. Pour a little oil on the top to seal it.

3 tbsp onion, finely chopped

3 tsp fresh root ginger, finely chopped

2 tsp ground rice

2 tsp white granulated sugar

2 tbsp hot bean paste or chilli sauce

2 cloves garlic, crushed

4 tbsp tomato purée (paste)

12 tbsp *Shaoxing* (rice) wine or medium sherry

3 tbsp brandy

Our Secret
Pre-prepared cook-in sauces are not really a Chinese tradition, unless you include the modern take-away tradition. They will never completely replace the subtle and fresh flavours coaxed into a classic stir fry through imagination and experience.

Duck Breasts in Red Wine Sediment Paste

Serves 2

2 duck breasts

2 tbsp chopped young leeks,

1 slice fresh root ginger

1 small clove garlic, chopped

2 tbsp wine sediment paste (see page 119)

1 tsp white granulated sugar

pinch of salt

2 tbsp *Shaoxing* (rice) wine or medium sherry

2 tsp dark soy sauce

Preheat the oven to 200ºC/400ºF/Gas 6. Gently dry-fry the duck breasts, skin side down, in a heavy-based pan until the skin shrinks a little and turns golden brown. Transfer to a shallow casserole.

Stir fry the leek, ginger and garlic in the remaining duck fat for 30 seconds, then add the wine sediment paste, sugar, salt, *Shaoxing* wine and soy sauce and mix together. Spoon the mixture over the duck.

Put the casserole in the oven and cook for 20–25 minutes, or until just cooked through. Cut the breasts across into slices about 1 cm/½ in thick to serve.

Our Secret
Meats cooked in wine sediment paste have such a distinctive flavour that they can be served as part of a cold platter or as a starter.

Sweet Yellow Bean Sauce

This is a sauce that can be used with all the dishes that come wrapped in pancake or crispy iceberg lettuce. Often misleadingly called 'plum sauce', it is our preference as the accompaniment to Peking Duck and Pancakes. Others simply smear on hoisin sauce or a kind of fermented wheat sauce, but this recipe is much superior.

Heat the oil in a small saucepan. When hot, add the yellow bean paste and stir over a low heat for 2–3 minutes. Add the sugar and 3 tablespoons of water and stir for another 2–3 minutes. Finally add the sesame oil and stir for a further 30 seconds.

2 tbsp vegetable or peanut oil

8 tbsp yellow bean paste

4 tbsp white granulated sugar

1 tsp sesame oil

Our Secret
Hoisin sauce creamed together with a little sesame paste and sesame oil is a great dip for plain cooked meats. At home we would always be served Sunday roasted meats on Mondays with all manner of savoury condiments. Once stored in a sealed jar you can keep *hoisin* in the refrigerator for months. If it dries simply add a little oil.

Yuxiang Sauce

6 tsp white sugar

2 tsp Sichuan peppercorns, roasted and crushed

2 tsp black pepper

2 tbsp light soy sauce

2 tbsp dark soy sauce

4 tbsp *Zhengjiang*, red wine or balsamic vinegar

1 tbsp cornflour (cornstarch) dissolved in 4 tbsp water

1 tbsp hot bean paste or chilli sauce

12 tbsp vegetable oil

12 slices fresh root ginger, finely chopped

12 small spring onions (scallions), finely chopped

12 medium cloves garlic, peeled and mashed

Since yuxiang (pronounced yoo syang) translates as 'fish fragrance' or 'fishy', it doesn't often get translated and remains on the menu as yuxiang. In fact the translation fails to convey its real meaning which is simply the combination of spring onion (scallion), ginger, vinegar and garlic which are the best seasonings for fish. Ginger neutralises the fishiness, which is not thought to be an attribute. Since this sauce originates in Sichuan it also has the obligatory mala chilli and Sichuan pepper hot spice.

Mix the sugar, Sichuan peppercorns, pepper, soy sauces, vinegar, cornflour mixture and hot bean paste together.

Heat the wok over a high heat. Add the oil. When it just begins to smoke scatter in the ginger, spring onions and garlic. Turn for a moment in the oil. Pour in the sauces and bring to the boil. Keep stirring until the sauce thickens (about 2 minutes).

Our Secret
Far from being confined to dressing seafood and fish, *yuxiang* sauce is great with many vegetables, with pre-marinaded and seared chicken, pork or rabbit. Once prepared this sauce will keep for up to a week in the refrigerator. You can sear the meat or vegetables as in a standard stir fry then simmer it in the *yuxiang* sauce until the ingredients are cooked. Different meats and vegetables will need varying amounts of fluid, so add stock, water or *Shaoxing* wine to your taste.

Yuxiang Aubergine (Eggplant)

Aubergine is absolutely delicious served with the yuxiang *sauce. The garlic is meant to be especially strong in this dish. Serve with rice or tossed with noodles.*

Heat the oil in a wok until it begins to smoke. Add the garlic and turn in the oil for a couple of seconds. Quickly add the aubergine (eggplant) and turn together briskly for 2 minutes.

Add the *yuxiang* sauce and 2 tablespoons of water and bring to the boil. Turn the heat down and simmer until the liquid has reduced (about 6 minutes), adding more water if the sauce begins to crackle and dry.

Serves 2–3

3 tbsp vegetable oil

4 large cloves garlic, peeled and crushed

1 large aubergine (eggplant), cut into small cubes

8 tbsp *yuxiang* sauce (see previous page)

Our Secrets

It is important not to burn the garlic. Simply toss the garlic into the wok so that it releases its flavour into the hot oil. Then immediately throw in the aubergine so that its moisture hydrates the garlic and prevents it from getting too hot or sticking to the pan.

We like to slice the aubergine, but it is more traditionally Chinese to skin and dice it. The traditional way gives a mushy consistency, but also avoids that characteristic bitterness that Chinese dislike.

Sesame Sauce

1 tbsp dark soy sauce

1 tbsp light soy sauce

4 tbsp sesame paste or dark tahini

white granulated sugar, to taste

2 tbsp *Shaoxing* (rice) wine or medium sherry

½ tbsp of the juice from a jar of red fermented bean curd

½ tbsp shrimp or fish sauce

2 cloves garlic, crushed and finely chopped

1 tbsp hot bean paste or chilli sauce

1 tbsp *hoisin* sauce

1 tbsp finely chopped mixed Chinese chives (*jui cai*), coriander (cilantro) and spring onions (scallions)

This is a magic sauce that we always keep in the refrigerator ready to spoon on to fresh Italian pasta or rice with a little coriander (cilantro), julienned cucumber and chopped spring onions (scallions). Or, serve it with raw vegetables as a crudité. It's a big hit with children, who are familiar with the nutty taste from peanut butter, but for them it may be better to reduce the amount of hot bean paste and add a little stock or water. The crisp moist taste of the vegetables or the blandness of the rice and pasta is essential to contrast with this sauce.

Beat the soy sauces with the sesame paste until well mixed. Then stir in the remaining ingredients.

Our Secret

It is also possible to stir fry with sesame paste. Chicken or pork are especially suitable. Simply sear the meat by deep-frying or steaming until it changes colour. Then stir fry it together with the sauce and a complementary vegetable. Depending on the consistency of your sauce you might need to add more stock or water.

Bang Bang Chicken

Sichuan Bang Bang Chicken is similar to Gado Gado in Indonesian cookery. Sesame is used a great deal in Sichuan cuisine, as is chilli. With the combination of cucumber and chilli there is a delicious contrast of both cold and hot tossed together. This dish is so simple to prepare and most of it can be prepared in advance.

Sprinkle the cucumber with salt and chill for 20 minutes. Squeeze off any excess liquid.

Bring enough water to cover the chicken breasts to the boil. Add the meat, leek and ginger, then bring back to the boil. Turn down the heat immediately and simmer gently for 15–20 minutes, or until the chicken is just cooked through. Turn the breast to prevent it from drying out. Set aside.

When the chicken has cooled, shred it along the grain into long thin pieces. Line a dish with the watercress or the noodles. Spread the cucumber as a bed on the dish and pile the shredded chicken on top in a mound. Decorate with slivers of pepper.

At the last minute, spoon the sauce evenly over the chicken. Toss everything together at the table before serving, hot or cold.

Serves 4 as a side dish or starter

240 g/8 oz medium cucumber, halved lengthways, seeded, then cut into 7.5 cm/3 in sections and shredded

pinch of salt

240 g/8 oz chicken breast

1 small, young leek, roughly chopped

2 slices fresh root ginger

bunch of watercress or 180 g/6 oz prepared rice noodles to serve

10 tbsp sesame sauce (see previous page)

slivers of red pepper to garnish

Our Secret
If you keep some prepared sesame sauce it is great for serving with leftover roast chicken – simply toss it with some blanched vegetables and noodles.

Black Bean Sauce

1 tbsp vegetable oil

2 large cloves garlic, coarsely chopped

2 tbsp fermented black beans, roughly chopped and soaked in hot water for 10 minutes

3 slices fresh root ginger, coarsely chopped

1 large spring onion (scallion)

2 tbsp dark soy sauce

2 tbsp *Shaoxing* (rice) wine or medium sherry

2 heaped tsp white granulated sugar

175 ml/6 fl oz/¾ cup water or chicken stock

Black beans were one of the innovations of the late warring states and early Imperial period of China. The fermentation and decomposition process, which is interrupted to heat and blacken the beans at a high temperature, was a great leap forward in Chinese cuisine and the one that began the ascent of the indigestible plain soy bean to the staple that it is today.

Heat the oil in the wok until it just begins to smoke. Scatter the garlic, black beans, ginger and spring onion in the oil and turn together to explode the flavours. Then add the remaining ingredients and bring to the boil. Turn down the heat and simmer for 5 minutes.

Our Secret

The secret of cooking in black bean sauce is to stir or deep-fry the meat or vegetable first momentarily, then remove it from the pan and set aside. Stir the dry ingredients for the sauce into the hot oil for a few seconds to explode the flavours. Then quickly add the remaining sauce ingredients and simmer together. Finally return the meat or vegetable to the pan.

Chilli Beef with Black Bean Sauce

This recipe adds a little chilli to fire up the beef. To serve in traditional restaurant style you will need to buy an iron plate which you heat in the oven and then place in a wooden base. These are commonly available in Chinese supermarkets and look very attractive at the table. The sauce continues to bubble, crackle and steam as you serve it piping hot.

Sprinkle the meat with salt, rubbing it in. Mix the cornflour (cornstarch) with the egg and 1 tablespoon of oil until well blended. Coat the beef evenly with the batter. Heat the iron plate.

Heat the remaining oil in a frying pan (skillet). When hot, add the beef and stir fry quickly for 1½ minutes or until all the meat has changed colour. Scoop out the beef and set aside. Scatter the peppers and chilli into the pan and turn in the oil for 15 seconds. Add the sauce and heat through. Return the beef to the pan and turn and stir with the remaining ingredients. Pour on to the pre-heated iron plate and serve immediately. ·

Serves 6

640 g/1¼ lb beef steak (topside, rump, fillet or sirloin), cut into 5 cm x 2.5 cm/2 in x 1 in slivers

1 tsp salt

1 tbsp cornflour (cornstarch)

1 egg

4½ tbsp vegetable oil

1 large spring onion (scallion), finely chopped

1 medium (bell) pepper, cut into 2 cm x 3 cm/¾ in x 1¼ in pieces

2–3 chillies, seeded and shredded

10 tbsp black bean sauce (see opposite page)

Our Secret

Once the sauce has been prepared and cooled you can pour a little cold oil over the top and keep it for up to a week in the refrigerator. When you are ready to use it simply sear the meat first. Then stir fry any vegetables and add the sauce, finally returning the meat to the pan. You can see a variation on this sauce below and in Black Bean Seafood where it is combined with prawns, squid and mussels; or simply pour the sauce over a whole fish before you steam it. For vegetables such as broccoli, stir fry the florets and then steam for a while in a little sauce, turning constantly while the sauce reduces.

Sweet and Sour Hot Bean Sauce

6 large Chinese dried mushrooms

4 tbsp vegetable oil

4 dried chillies

½ red (bell) pepper, diced

1 carrot, diced

2 green chillies, seeded and shredded

3 slices fresh root ginger, finely chopped

2 large cloves garlic, crushed and chopped

½ tsp salt

5 tbsp light soy sauce

8 tbsp reduced stock

6 tbsp *zhangjiang* vinegar

3 tbsp white granulated sugar

1 tbsp hot bean paste or chilli sauce

2 tbsp *Shaoxing* (rice) wine or medium sherry

1 x 8 oz can crushed pineapple or pineapple chunks in its own juice, finely chopped

2 spring onions (scallions), finely chopped

1 tbsp sesame oil

1 tbsp cornflour (cornstarch) blended with 2 tbsp water

This is our hybrid version of sweet and sour, which for the 'foreign devils' might be served with chicken or pork, but has traditionally been a dressing for fish. It's sweet and sour and hot without any of the flavours dominating.

Soak the mushrooms in hot water for 30 minutes, remove the hard stalks and slice the caps. Heat the oil in the wok and turn the dried chillies in the oil. Add the rest of the vegetables (except the spring onions) and ginger, garlic and salt. Stir fry together for 1 minute.

Add the soy sauce, stock, vinegar, sugar, hot bean paste and wine. Bring to the boil, stirring constantly. Turn the heat down. Add the pineapple juice. Finally stir in the pineapple and scatter in the spring onions and glaze with sesame oil. Add the cornflour paste just before serving (see Our Secret below).

Our Secret

You can cool and store the sauce in a sealed jar for a week or more. When you are ready to use, heat it through, add the cornflour mixture (or an amount of cornflour appropriate to the amount of sauce you are about to use), stirring to keep smooth until the sauce thickens.

Home-style Fried Rice (page 106)

Lamb in Cumin Sesame Cream Sauce (page 36) and Laobing (page 112)

Stir-fried Cauliflower (page 80) and

Chicken and Chestnut Casserole (page 35)

Radish and Carrot Pickle (page 84) and Lamb with Sichuan Peppercorns (page 46)

Chicken Steamed in Lotus Leaves (page 50)

Sea Bass with Sweet and Sour Hot Bean Sauce

This is an attempt to recreate a dish served in a restaurant behind the Drum Tower in Beijing. It makes a good centre spread with a few more minor dishes to be served with rice. By pressing the fish down upright against the base of the oil you can get it to look like it is leaping and twisting on the dish. To be really fancy serve it leaping on a bed of bak choy or spinach.

Clean and scale the fish, leaving the head and tail on. Make a slit from the belly to the tip of the tail, exposing the bone. Make two deep cuts on the fat part of its belly. Rub the fish inside and out with salt. Beat the egg. Dust the fish with cornflour (cornstarch). Rub in the beaten egg and then coat it with flour. (Cook the bak choy and arrange it on the dish as if the white bulbs were waves).

Make sure that you have a ring base for your wok or a flat bottom wok that is stable on the cooker. Heat the oil in the wok over a high heat. Carefully place the fish into the oil manoeuvring it with a couple of metal spatulas. Carefully manoeuvre it so it is upright and press down in the middle of the back. Its two sides should splay out to either side. Keep up the pressure while continuously basting the fish with the oil. After a minute the fish should be quite firm.

Turn the heat down to medium and continue to cook gently for a further 4 minutes, pressing and basting. Meanwhile, heat the sauce in a separate pan, adding the cornflour. Turn the heat up again for the last minute and serve the fish with the sauce drizzled all over it, or in a separate sauce boat if you prefer.

Serves 2

1 small sea bass
(about 400 g/14 oz)

1 tsp salt

1 egg

cornflour (cornstarch) for dusting

60 g/2 oz/½ cup plain (all-purpose) flour

oil for deep-frying

250 ml/8 fl oz/1 cup sweet and sour hot bean sauce (see opposite page)

bak choy to decorate the plate

Our Secret

We love this sauce stir fried with monkfish, which holds its shape and so lends itself to the rigours of stir fry techniques. Simply marinate thickly sliced fillets with ginger and wine and then sear them in hot oil. Heat the sauce, mixing with a little *Shaoxing* wine to get a good consistency and return the fish to the pan, coating it with sauce.

Desserts

Sweet delights to be treasured

We have chosen to place the dessert chapter before the end of the book because sweet food does not normally bring the Chinese banquet or meal to an end. Instead, one or two sweet courses are included in the procession of savoury courses. Thus if you order blindly from a menu, only offered in Chinese, the chances are that several dishes will be sweet.

Often the sweetness will come in the form of a vegetable or bean-based dish. Red beans (aduki) are most popular and to be found in many of the steamed and deep-fried rice doughs and pastries. Sometimes a sweet dish, like Eight Treasure Pudding will punctuate a meal, or a sweet soup will freshen the palate in readiness for the next courses.

Lychees and longyan (dragon's eyes), kumquats, pears and white fungus may all come served in a sweetened water, and flavoured with ginger or cassia flowers. We should not assume that Chinese sweets, cakes and confectioneries are limited in range. Chinese markets and temple fairs overflow with dried fruits and little cakes steamed, stuffed, deep-fried and baked. Many are a form of dimsum made with steamed sweet pastes. And Northerners prefer caramelised sweets speared on long cocktail sticks and served in a range of nuts and fruit that put our toffee apples to shame.

If you find it difficult to conclude a meal with soup, as the Chinese do, you can finish with a plate of delicately sliced fruits served on ice and eaten with cocktail sticks. For an exotic fruit salad see our Dragon's Eye Fruit Salad served in melon, or simply serve quartered oranges as they do in most Chinese restaurants.

Apple and Walnut Treat

This used to be available on the streets of Beijing. These days you can still find caramelised crab apples and haw apples, but we have only ever read about them being sold interspersed with walnuts. This is our recreation of the traditional snack. Crab apples' tart flavour contrasts sharply with the toffee (taffy), but as most people don't have crab apple trees we have substituted cooking apples.

Mix the flour with 120 ml/4 fl oz/½ cup cold water and beaten egg. Beat to a smooth batter. Cut each apple into quarters and then half once more.

Prepare the toffee coating in two batches. Heat a wide based pan over a high heat and then add the oil, swirl it around the pan and then turn the heat down. Pour in half the sugar and 4 tablespoons of water. Do not stir or the mixture will go hard and granular. When it foams, pass a spoon through the sugar water to check that it has melted, then turn the heat up a little. The mixture will turn golden brown. Be careful not to let the sugar burn.

Meanwhile, quickly dip the apple pieces in the batter, then sprinkle with sesame seeds. Heat the vegetable oil for deep-frying in a wok. Fry the battered apple pieces in batches for 2½ minutes. Drain.

When all the apple pieces have been fried and drained, spear three pieces of apple alternately with three walnuts on a satay stick. Then dip each stick one at a time into the hot sugar coating. Coat thoroughly, then dip quickly into a bowl of ice-cold water. Make up another batch of the toffee coating and repeat until the apples and walnuts are used up.

Serves 3–4

For the batter:

100 g/3½ oz plain/scant 1 cup (all-purpose) flour

1 egg, beaten

4 medium cooking apples or 500 g/1 lb crab apples, peeled and cored

3 tbsp vegetable or peanut oil

500 g/1lb white granulated sugar

2 tbsp sesame seeds

210 g/7 oz walnuts

vegetable oil for deep-frying

You will also need:

20 cm/8 in satay sticks

Our Secret
For years, this dessert seemed impossible to get right, but the trick is in not stirring the sugar while you are heating it. Adding 2 teaspoons of water also helps the sugar turn to syrup. You must work quickly to stop the sugar hardening. The sugar should turn a golden brown, but don't let the caramel burn or the result will be bitter.

Eight Treasure Pudding

Serves 6–8

590 g/1 lb 3 oz glutinous rice

4 tbsp vegetable oil

3 tbsp white granulated sugar

300 g/10 oz red bean paste

lard or butter for greasing

30 g/1 oz walnuts

6 tbsp juicy dried apricots and other dried fruits

This is the classic party pudding. We serve it at the New Year festival. Many of the dried fruits, like angelica, have therapeutic qualities and the red bean paste is a tonic thought to nourish the heart. Being well steamed, the pudding is also easy to digest, so you can also serve this for the old and sick as restorative food.

Wash the rice and place in a saucepan. Cover with 1 cm/½ in water. Bring to the boil and simmer gently for 30 minutes, adding more water if it seems to be sticking. Add the oil and sugar, turn and stir until well mixed.

Meanwhile, soften the red bean paste by placing in a pan of hot water for 30 minutes. Grease the sides of a large heatproof basin or bowl heavily with the fat. Stick the nuts and candied or dried fruits in a pattern on the sides and bottom of the basin. Divide the rice into four portions and the bean paste into three portions.

Place a layer of sweetened rice in the basin, then spread a thinner layer of red bean paste on top of the rice. Repeat the layers, finishing with a rice layer and packing the mixture down into the bowl. Cover the basin and refrigerate.

When the pudding is needed, place the basin into a covered steamer and steam steadily for at least 1½ hours, as you would cook Christmas pudding. Invert the basin on to a large round heated serving dish. Decorate with extra fruit.

Our Secret

Prepare your Eight Treasure Pudding in advance as the un-steamed pudding will mature for up to four days in the refrigerator.

Eight Treasure Tea

This is one of the few teas automatically served alongside a meal. These eight treasures are all commonly used in traditional Chinese medicine and the combination is designed to make you live for ever. Rock sugar gives the tea a subtle sweetness, counteracted by a slightly tart touch from the hawthorn and wolfberries. All of these ingredients are easily found in a good Chinese supermarket, but may not be marked with the English translation. The ingredients on the first list should be included, but you can vary the others.

For each cup, combine a small pinch of tea, one small head of chrysanthemum (more will dominate), 10 *gou qi zi*, one 1 cm/½ in cube of rock sugar with a combination of four of the other ingredients. Just use 1 piece of each of the ingredients in the second list, and 2 or 3 raisins.

Pour on half a cup of boiling water and cover. Leave to infuse for 10 minutes then fill with more boiling water.

Essentials:

tea (jasmine or black tea)

dried chrysanthemum

gou qi zi, (Chinese wolf berry) pronounced 'goh chee dz'

rock sugar

Plus, a selection of the following:

long gan (dried longan pulp)

red dates

raisins

walnuts

lotus nuts (round white nuts)

shan zha, pronounced 'shan jar' or dried slices of hawthorn berry

Our Secret
Traditional restaurants in Beijing have one waiter brandishing a shiny copper kettle with a spout that seems to be several feet long. His job is to keep your cup filled with freshly boiled water without jostling up to the table. Unlike infusions of black tea, Eight Treasure Tea gets better the longer you leave it to infuse. Keep filling up the cup as you drink. One infusion will last all night.

Sweet Almond 'Soup'

Serves 3

210 g/7 oz ground
almonds

20 g/¾ oz glutinous rice
powder or plain ground
rice

sugar, to taste

*Here is a substantial sweet and thin rice porridge that was often
peddled on the streets of old Beijing at daybreak.*

Put the almonds and rice powder in a blender or food processor.
With the motor running, slowly add 1 litre/¾ pints/4 cups water to
make a liquid. Pour into a pan and add sugar to taste.

Place over a medium heat and simmer for 10 minutes, stirring to
prevent it sticking. Add more water if the mixture thickens too much.
Serve in small bowls for breakfast.

Our Secret
For a lighter breakfast 'tea', which you can store for a while in the
refrigerator, soak the almonds in boiling water until the soaking water
has cooled. Pour off the water and repeat the whole process three
times. Then grind and mash the almonds and mix them well with four
times their weight of warm runny honey. To serve, add one
dessertspoon of the mixture to a mug for each person and pour on
boiling water.

Red Bean Sticky Rice Roll

Here we have a traditional spring or moon festival cake. In May they are thrown into the river to commemorate the story of the exiled scholar and official Qu yuan who, believing that his king was beguiled by corrupt advisers, commited suicide by jumping into the Miluo river in grief and protest. The fish, having eaten the cakes, will leave the body of Qu Yuan!

Mix the sugar and sesame seeds. Place the rice in a heatproof dish in a pan of water. Cover and steam for about 1 hour until well cooked and sticky. Pound the cooked rice with a pestle for five minutes until it becomes smooth and doughy.

Dust a work surface with half the sesame and sugar. Roll and press out the rice dough into a 30 cm x 20 cm/12 in x 8 in sheet 2.5 cm/ 1 in thick.

Roll out the bean paste on top of the dough. Then take both the short sides and fold them to meet in the centre and then fold in half along the central join, taking care not to break the rice layer.

Sprinkle the remaining sesame mixture all over the folded dough. Then cut the envelope into about 10 pieces roughly 2.5 cm/1 in thick.

Serves 10

60 g/2 oz/¼ cup caster sugar

150 g/5 oz sesame powder or ground sesame seeds, toasted and ground

500 g/1 lb glutinous rice, soaked in 450ml/¾ pint/ scant 2 cups cold water for 2 hours

240 g/8 oz red bean paste

Our Secrets

If you wet your hands, it makes the sticky dough much easier to manipulate.

To make the filling more fragrant, mix 60 g/2 oz creamy sesame paste with the red bean paste. If you can find cassia blossoms they are also a traditional ingredient for this filling.

Coconut Cake

Serves 10

4 egg whites

15 g/½ oz agar agar

2 x 400 ml cans coconut milk

150 g/5 oz/¾ cup white granulated sugar

30 g/1 oz gelatine or gelatine substitute dissolved in a little hot water

We started off selling almond junket (see page 130) in our restaurant – a personal favourite – but found that our customers were not unanimously in agreement. After scouring Chinatown for a cake that would be acceptable to our customers we settled upon this coconut version. Chef Tim Diep came up with the recipe below. Serve with fresh fruit salad made from kiwi fruit, strawberries, melons and perhaps some canned lychees.

Whip the egg whites until stiff and frothy. Bring 600ml/1 pint/2½ cups water to the boil, then add the agar agar. Stir and simmer for 5 minutes. Add the coconut milk, sugar and gelatine, and re-heat, stirring until the ingredients are mixed thoroughly. Do not boil.

Strain and discard the tough pieces of agar agar. Leave to cool until it just begins to set. Fold in the egg white. Refrigerate until ready to use. Cut into slabs and serve with fresh fruit salad.

Our Secret

Vegetarians can use agar agar instead of gelatine, although it takes experience to know how to use it and often leads to a more blancmange-like consistency. Some of the powdered agar agar or gelatine substitutes available in health food shops are more reliable.

Almond Junket

This light junket is a perfect summer dessert and especially attractive with fresh fruit salad.

If the almonds are whole, blanch them briefly in boiling water. Then grind in a blender or with a mortar and pestle. Add 900 ml/ 1½ pints/3¾ cups water to the ground almonds, little by little, mixing slowly. Bring to the boil, then simmer for 5 minutes.

Add the agar agar and simmer for 2 minutes. Stir in the gelatine and sugar and continue to simmer until dissolved. Strain through a sieve. Add the almond extract and evaporated milk.

Pour into a shallow dish and refrigerate for about four hours. It should keep for about 4 days. The junket can be cut into diamonds or squares and should be served with a mixed fruit salad – perhaps kiwi fruit, strawberries or melon with a few canned lychees or loquats.

210 g/7 oz whole or ground almonds

15 g/½ oz agar agar

20 g/¾ oz gelatine

3 tbsp white granulated sugar

1 tsp almond extract (essence)

100 ml/3½ fl oz/scant 1 cup evaporated milk

Our Secret
Father used to make almond junket by adding gelatine to the almond tea recipe and replacing the extra water with evaporated milk. This makes a richer, heavier junket than the one we have included here.

Honey Pears

Serves 6

6 large, firm (but not hard)
conference pears

4 tbsp runny honey

4 tbsp ginger wine

In old China peaches were the fruits of the immortals. But they never savoured the delights of British pears. Here is one of father's recipes with a gingery twist.

Cut the tops from the pears about 2.5 cm/1 in below the stem. Reserve for the lids. Peel and core the pears from the top, leaving a good thick base. Stand them upright in a heatproof dish.

Blend the honey with the ginger wine and pour over and inside the pears. Replace the 'lids'.

Steam for 30 minutes, occasionally spooning the sauce over them. Refrigerate the pears for 1 hour. Serve with the honey sauce drizzled over them.

Our Secret
It is important to use pears that are neither too soft, nor too hard. They should be sweet to taste and maintain their firmness during the steaming process.

Dragon's Eye Fruit Salad

Most Chinese banquets end with fresh fruit to pick at, often served on a bed of ice. Here is a fruit salad with a difference – one that you can serve even in the depths of winter. The ginger and honey will be warming and therapeutic.

Drain the mandarin oranges, reserving their juice. Bring the juice gently to the boil with the ginger and honey. Then simmer and reduce until you have a runny syrup. Cool and refrigerate.

Cut the melons in half and discard the seeds, scoop out the flesh with a spoon so that it makes round balls. Reserve the melon skins.

Combine all the fruits and place inside the melon skins. Pour on the cooled syrup and replace the melon lid. Serve ½ melon per person.

Serves 4

240 g/8 oz canned mandarin oranges in natural juice

4 slices fresh root ginger

2 tbsp Acacia honey

2 small charartais, cantaloupe or galia melons

2–3 kiwi fruit, peeled and sliced

240 g/8 oz fresh *long gan* ('dragon's eyes'), or lychess, peeled and stoned

Our Secret
The fruits in this selection are all soft rather than crisp, even so they have very different textures that complement each other. You can vary the fruits, bearing in mind that it is important to keep the variety of texture, colour and the mixture of different sweet flavours, the mellow, tart and bland.

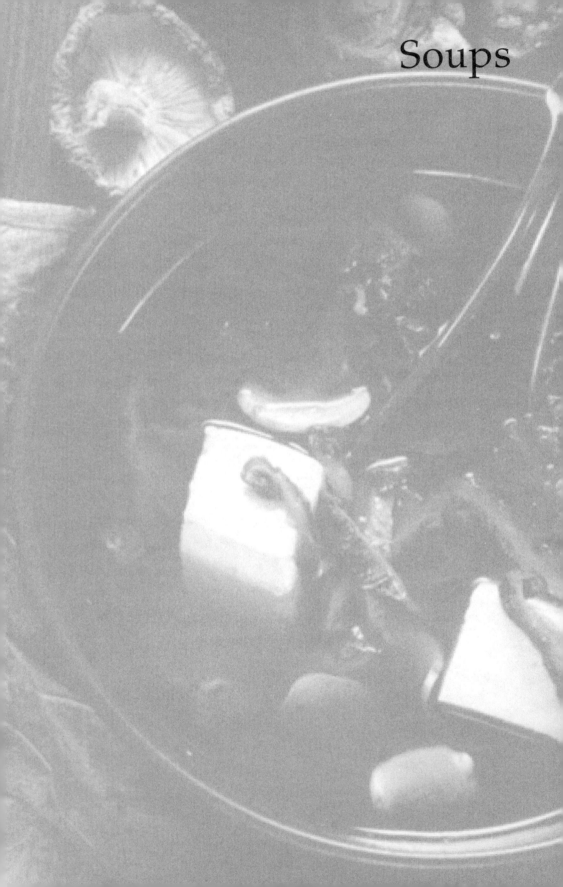

The end of the journey

Chinese soups fulfil many different functions and should not be thought of as a simple starter. Often, soup is served last, which is why the soup chapter brings this book to a close. Many are served with noodles, as a meal-in-one with blanched vegetables and griddled meats arranged on the surface.

Some soups, such as those that are simply poached vegetables served with the boiling water, are almost indistinguishable from hot water. This is because they really are only enhanced hot water taken to help the rice dishes go down smoothly. Nanny Ding's Soup is just such a hot water soup, lightly flavoured with tomatoes and fresh coriander (cilantro). Delicious sweet soups often conclude a meal in the manner of a dessert – and sometimes make a light breakfast.

Simple Stock Making

One of the most frustrating conundrums of this book is that many of our dishes specify freshly made stock. There is no doubt that if you are making a clear soup there is nothing comparable to the broths described below, but if you are simply adding a tablespoon or two to a stir fry you can use ready prepared stock powder or simply water. A quick way to get a good chicken stock for two is to buy a chicken leg and breast together. Remove the breast for cooking, but boil the leg with some ginger, radish and spring onions (scallions) for 20 minutes or more. Another tip is to freeze unused stock in an ice cube tray so that you always have small amounts available.

Vegetarian bouillon powders, now commonly available in health food shops, are much better than they used to be, but the dominant flavour is still salt. If you like a seafood flavour, Japanese bonito flakes may be to your taste.

The following stocks are used for a variety of recipes, but if served as soup they will provide for 4 people.

Basic Chicken Stock

There is nothing like a golden home-made chicken broth. To get the most out of the chicken use a whole one then remove the best bits after 30 minutes for use in a recipe that requires pre-cooked chicken.

Remove the fat from the cavity and cut off the parson's nose. Rinse the chicken in cold water. Slice through the chicken at the wing and leg joints and chop the wings and legs into 2.5 cm/1 in pieces. Chop the chicken through lengthwise to separate the breast from the back. Chop the back into two pieces lengthways and then chop these into 2.5 cm/1 in pieces. Peel the ginger and cut into thick slices. Wash and trim the carrots and spring onions.

Place the pork bones and all the chicken except the breast into a large heavy pan. Cover it with water and bring to a brisk boil. Turn off the heat immediately and strain, pouring the water away.

Return the cleaned bones to the pan with the vegetables and the remaining ingredients. Pour on 4.5 litres/8 pints/20 cups water and bring to a brisk boil. Add the chicken breast. Turn heat to low and skim off all the impurities from the surface.

When the liquid is clear, turn heat higher and boil again. Adjust to a gentle simmer, preventing the stock from coming to a full boil. After 30 minutes remove the breast and cut the meat from the bones. Return the bones to the tureen. Simmer for a further 3 hours, stirring occasionally and skimming the surface to keep the broth clear.

Cool, then strain through muslin (cheesecloth). Discard the meat and bones. Repeat the straining. Skim the fat from the stock if it is to be used straight away. Season lightly to taste with salt. The stock will keep for 4–5 days in the refrigerator and for longer in the freezer. Leave the fat on the top to seal the jar. Bring the stock to the boil again before using.

1 large free-range chicken

3 cm/1¼ in piece fresh root ginger

4 large carrots

4 large spring onions (scallions)

500 g/1 lb pork bones

salt and sugar to taste

60 g/2 oz stalks from Chinese dried mushrooms, rinsed (optional)

1 tsp white peppercorns

dash of oyster sauce (optional)

Our Secret

In the winter, you can put some *Huang Qi* (radix astralagus) into the stock, because it is a fortifying herb.

Vegetarian Stock

1 large Chinese white
radish (daikon)

4 large carrots

handful of coriander
(cilantro) and parsley
stalks

60 g/2 oz Chinese dried
mushroom stalks, rinsed
(optional)

4 cm/1½ in piece fresh root
ginger

2 bay leaves

salt and sugar to taste

bouillon powder to taste
(optional)

Here is a clear vegetarian stock for the Spring Vegetable Noodle Soup or any other dish that requires vegetable stock. Be careful not to use ingredients like celery which give the stock a turbid colour. We often add a pinch of ready-made stock powder as a tiny bit will pep up an uninteresting stock or a soup made quickly with lightly poached vegetables like spinach or watercress.

Wash and trim the vegetables and peel the ginger, cutting it into thick slices. Put all the ingredients in a large pan with 3 litres/5 pints/ 12½ cups water.

Bring the water to a vigorous boil, then turn the heat down, skimming any impurities from the surface. Simmer for 3 hours, uncovered, then strain through muslin (cheesecloth) or a fine sieve. Season lightly to taste with salt, remembering that there will be further seasoning when the final soup is prepared. If you eat fish, a dash of fish sauce is a good, delicate addition to the broth.

Our Secrets

When making a stock you do not need to think about the quantity you are making because you adapt and adjust it according to your needs, and you can add ingredients to fortify it or water to dilute it at any time.

In general, it is better not to make a stock too strong with the bouillon powder so that the flavour of the vegetables can be released, but it is a useful means of improving a soup whose flavour is a little weak.

Fish Stock

Unlike the other stocks which serve multiple purposes, fish stock should only be used for fish or seafood soups and stir fry sauces. This recipe produces a delicately flavoured broth, perfect for preparing a light soup to serve inbetween courses or at the end of a meal.

Slice the vegetables and ginger and lay on top of the fish bones in a large pan. Add the remaining ingredients and 1½ litres/2½ pints/ 6¼ cups water. Bring to the boil.

Simmer for 45 minutes. Skim off the froth and strain. Reduce to 1 litre/½ pint by simmering with the lid off.

Enhanced Stocks

To enhance any of these stocks simply reduce it to half the volume by simmering with the pan lid off.

2 onions

3 carrots

3 leeks

2 celery sticks

2.5 cm/1 in piece fresh root ginger

4 plaice or sole bones (no heads)

6 black peppercorns

1 tbsp oyster sauce

1 head star anise

Our Secret
We like to add salted cabbage to this stock sometimes because it adds a strong, savoury flavour.

Nanny Ding's Light Vegetable Soup

Serves 2

½ tbsp vegetalbe oil

3 large slices fresh
root ginger

2 young leeks, sliced
lengthways, then shredded
finely on the diagonal

2 tomatoes, peeled

pinch of salt and white
pepper

1 litre/1¾ pints/4 cups
spring water

handful of coriander
(cilantro) leaves, chopped

1 x 125 g carton of silken
bean curd, cut into
small cubes

This light, clear soup is at the top end of the range, both quick to prepare and the nearest to drinking hot water flavoured lightly with vegetables and coriander. Given the simple, unadulterated flavours it is best to use pure, still spring water. This is not a soup to start a meal. Use it on fasting days, after a period of excess or to cool yourself in mid-summer. Traditionally you might find this kind of soup between courses or at the end of a banquet.

Heat the oil in a heavy pan and scatter in the ginger and leek. Turn together for 1 minute. Add the tomatoes and seasoning, gently breaking the tomatoes up. Pour in the water.

Bring to the boil and allow to simmer for a further 1 minute until the leeks are soft and the tomato has disintegrated. Add the coriander and bean curd. Return to the boil, then simmer for 30 seconds.

Our Secret
If you don't have bean curd, drizzle one beaten egg white into the soup. This gives the stock the appearance of striated clouds.

Chicken Soup with Noodles

Every self-respecting culture has a version of chicken soup to come home to. This is our easy interpretation of the Chinese version – lean, clean and green, without being insipid. Preserved cabbage (snow pickle) is salted greens that you can buy in cans at any Chinese supermarket. Be sure to distinguish it from zha cai, *the knobbly Sichuan pickle, that is preserved in chilli. Light and easy to digest it is a perfect lunchtime dish and no wonder that chicken noodle soup is the Oriental choice on fashionable menus.*

Soak the mushrooms in hot water for 30 minutes, remove the hard stalks and finely slice the caps. Combine the marinade ingredients, then rub this mixture into the chicken. Leave for 15 minutes.

Heat the oil in a wide heavy frying pan (skillet) or griddle pan. Place the chicken on top and press down with a spatula. Cook it until golden brown and then turn over and repeat. Make sure the chicken is cooked right through.

Meanwhile, heat the mushrooms and cabbage on the other side of the pan. Keep turning to heat through. Sprinkle liberally with pepper.

Boil the egg noodles for 30 seconds and place in a large soup bowl. Pour on the hot stock. Arrange the chicken, mushroom and pickle on top of the soup.

Serves 1

3 Chinese dried mushrooms

120 g/4 oz/½ cup chicken breast cut across the grain into strips 2.5 cm/1 in long

½ tbsp vegetable oil

small handful of preserved cabbage (snow pickle)

white pepper to taste

120 g/4oz/½ cup fresh egg noodles

400 ml/14fl oz/1⅔ cups hot chicken stock

For the marinade:

1 tsp sesame oil

½ tsp cornflour (cornstarch)

½ tsp white granulated sugar

1 tsp *Shaoxing* (rice) wine or medium sherry

pinch of pepper

pinch of salt

Our Secrets

Chicken noodle soup has been a tradition in our family for many generations. Great-grandmother's birthday was the occasion for inviting guests from all over the Min valley to a great banquet. The house was filled with yellow and orange chrysanthemums and as the guests entered the front door they were always welcomed with a tiny bowl of clear chicken noodle soup. For this kind of drinking soup you need more stock than chicken and noodles.

To make this soup for more people, increase the quantities of the ingredients by the number of serving sizes you want.

Spring Vegetable Noodle Soup

Serves 4–5

5 Chinese dried
mushrooms

15 g/½ oz wood ear

2 tbsp vegetable oil

2 cloves garlic, crushed

6 slices fresh root ginger,
finely chopped

60 g/2 oz young carrots,
thinly sliced

60 g/2 oz onions, sliced

18 mangetout, halved

½ red (sweet) pepper,
cored, seeded and sliced

½ green (sweet) pepper,
cored, seeded and sliced

120 g/4 oz beansprouts

30 g/1 oz each sliced
bamboo shoots and water
chestnuts

For stir frying:

pinch of salt

½ tsp white pepper

pinch of sugar

1 tbsp each light soy
sauce, vegetarian oyster
sauce, sesame oil and
Shaoxing (rice) wine

For each person:

300 ml/10 fl oz/1¼ cups
hot vegetable stock

120 g/4 oz fresh egg
noodles

chopped coriander
(cilantro), to garnish

Don't be put off by the number of ingredients in this recipe. You can vary the recipe to whatever you have at home. Simply be sensitive to the cooking time of each type of vegetable. If you are using a root make sure it is cut very finely, so it cooks quickly. It is essential to use a good stock. This is a light and cooling soup. Use it for when you're going into one of those lean periods, when you want to remedy excess, or in convalescence.

Heat the wok and add the oil. When it begins to smoke add the garlic, ginger and all the vegetables and turn in the oil for about 30 seconds. Add 2 tablespoons of stock, salt, pepper, sugar, light soy sauce and vegetarian oyster sauce and stir fry together for a couple of minutes. Finally add the sesame oil and *Shaoxing* wine. Turn together for another 30 seconds.

Boil the egg noodles for 1 minute. Drain and rinse the noodles under cold running water. Put the noodles in the hot stock for a few seconds, then divide among four large soup bowls. Pour on the stock. Arrange the vegetables on the surface of the soup. Garnish with coriander (cilantro).

Our Secret
A little freshly deep-fried Sichuan pickle (*zha cai*) will add chilli heat to the broth.

Pepperpot Fish

Watch out for the hot bean paste, this is a soup to make you sweat! If you like chillies but can't cope with too much, decrease the amount of sauce you use. This should be served between courses rather than as an appetiser.

Dust the fish with salt and cornflour and turn in the egg white.

Heat the wok and add the oil. When it smokes, add the coated fish and cook for 1 minute. Scoop out with a slotted spoon and keep warm.

Add the pickle to the wok and cook for 1 minute. Remove and drain, pour away the oil. Put the hot bean paste in the wok and stir it around.

Add the stock and bring to the boil in the saucepan with the pickle. Add the ginger and garlic and bring back to the boil for 1 minute. Add the fish, vinegar and pepper and simmer for 3–4 minutes. Finally add the bak choy and bring back to the boil. Simmer for a few seconds and serve in a heated bowl sprinkled with spring onions.

Serves 4

225 g/8 oz/1 cup white fish fillets, cut across into slices 4 cm x 2.5 cm/ 1½ in x 1 in

salt

1 tbsp cornflour (cornstarch)

2 egg whites, beaten

vegetable oil for deep-frying

1 tbsp Sichuan pickle (*zha cai*), chopped

2 tsp hot bean paste or chilli sauce

600 ml/1 pint/2½ cups chicken stock

2.5 cm/1 in piece fresh root ginger, finely shredded

1 clove garlic, finely sliced

2 tbsp white wine vinegar

½ tsp pepper

handful of bak choy or young spinach

1 spring onion (scallion), roughly chopped

Our Secret
There is something delightful about the unexpected – the inscrutable way that the unassuming white fish and bak choy in a clear stock explodes in your mouth. Develop the art of suprise in your cookery!

Chilli Beef Soup with River Noodles (*Hofun*)

Serves 3

For the marinade:

2 cloves garlic, crushed and finely chopped

pinch of salt

pinch of sugar

white pepper

1 tsp sesame oil

1 tsp hot bean paste

240 g/8 oz/1 cup rump or sirloin steak, sliced finely across the grain

3 Chinese dried mushrooms

½ tbsp vegetable oil

45 g/1½ oz mangetout

½ small red (bell) pepper, cored, seeded and sliced

½ small green (bell) pepper, cored, seeded and finely sliced

45 g/1½ oz Spanish onion, finely sliced

30 g/1 oz carrots

30 g/1 oz sliced bamboo shoots

30 g/1 oz sliced water chestnuts

45 g/1½ oz beansprouts

For each person:

180 g/6 oz fresh river noodles (*hofun*)

600 ml/1 pint/2½ cups enhanced hot beef stock

sesame oil and fresh chilli to garnish

This is one version of a soup that is a popular lunchtime snack in Beijing. The noodles should really be hand cut – where the chef holds a large block of dough on his shoulder and slices off fine slivers straight into the boiling stock.

Mix the marinade ingredients and coat the sliced beef. Leave overnight.

Soak the *hofun* in boiling water for a couple of minutes and then gently prise the slivers apart with your fingers.

Heat the wok and add the oil. When hot scatter in the beef and press down with a spatula. Cook until the meat has slightly browned, or to taste. Remove and set to one side. Then stir and toss all the vegetables in the oil. Add a couple of tablespoons of stock and bring to the boil. Place the noodles in a bowl and arrange the vegetables and griddled beef on top. Pour over the hot stock. Sprinkle with sesame oil and chilli.

Our Secret

For a hearty beef stock, make up the recipe as if for chicken stock, but with beef bones and add star anise, Sichuan pepper, onions, fresh ginger and wine.

Spinach and Silken Bean Curd Soup

This is one of those classic soups that would be served during or after a long banquet to aid digestion. It is a light soup that cooks early spring spinach quickly over a high heat to retain its nourishing and flavoursome qualities. The dark green spinach set against the white bean curd make a delightful springtime colour combination.

Wash the spinach thoroughly and blanch in boiling water. Rinse, squeeze dry and finely chop. Blanch the bean curd by soaking in boiling water for 10 minutes. Drain and leave to dry in a sieve.

Heat the oil in a wok over a high heat. Add the dried and fresh mushrooms and turn for 1 minute. Add the spinach, soy sauce and wine and stir for 30 seconds. Add the stock, cornflour paste, bean curd and salt and pepper. Bring back to the boil and simmer gently for 3–4 minutes. Sprinkle with sesame oil to serve.

Serves 4

150 g/5 oz young spinach

240 g/8 oz silken bean curd, cut into 2 cm/¾ in cubes and soaked in boiling water for 10 minutes

1 tbsp vegetable oil

4 Chinese dried mushrooms, soaked in hot water for 30 minutes, hard stalks removed and finely sliced

60 g/2 oz button mushrooms, finely sliced

1 tbsp light soy sauce

1 tbsp *Shaoxing* (rice) wine or medium sherry

600ml/1 pint/2½ cups enhanced stock

2 tsp cornflour (cornstarch) blended with a little water

½ tsp salt

pepper to taste

1 tsp sesame oil

Our Secret
If you find that the stock in this soup is too bland for your taste, add 1 teaspoon brown sugar.

Wun Tun Noodle Soup

Serves 20

Filling for 100 wun tun skins:

4 or 5 Chinese dried mushrooms

5 wood ears, soaked in hot water overnight, chopped

6 water chestnuts, finely chopped

6 strips of bamboo shoots, finely chopped

2 tbsp Chinese chives (*jiu cai*) or spring onions (scallions)

500 g/1 lb minced pork

210 g/7 oz prawns (shrimp), roughly chopped

1 tbsp *Shaoxing* (rice) wine or medium sherry

3 tsp sesame oil

½ tsp white granulated sugar

2 tsp salt

2 tsp pepper

2 tsp cornflour (cornstarch)

1 beaten egg white

100 wun tun skins

For each portion:

small handful spinach

300 ml/10 fl oz/1¼ cups enhanced chicken stock

90 g/3 oz fresh wun tun noodles

spring onions (scallions) and coriander (cilantro) to garnish

chilli sauce for dipping

Wun tun skins and noodles are widely available in Chinese supermarkets so we do not recommend trying to make them. Filling the dumplings is the kind of communal cooking that children love to help you with. It reminds them of paper folding and there is much fun to be had in the competition for the perfect dumpling. Prawns (shrimp) and Chinese chives are essential to the quality of taste and texture of the wun tun filling. Once you get the wun tun noodle soup bug, nothing else will do.

Soak the dried mushrooms in hot water for 30 minutes, remove the hard stalks then mince. Mix the mushrooms and wood ear with the water chestnuts, bamboo shoots, chives, pork and prawns (shrimp). Add the *Shaoxing* wine, sesame oil, sugar, salt, pepper, cornflour (cornstarch) and egg white and mix thoroughly.

Place a teaspoon of the stuffing on to the centre of the wun tun skin. Wet the edges and press together making a triangle. Take the two corners of the fold and bring them together again pressing and sticking them with a little water. Repeat with the remaining filling and wun tun skins. If you have made extra wun tuns these can be frozen.

Count 5 wun tun for each person and simmer in boiling water for 10 minutes. Meanwhile, boil a pan of water and simmer the wun tun noodles for two minutes. Blanch the greens. Heat the stock. Put the noodles in the bottom of a large soup bowl and pour over the stock. Arrange the greens and wun tun on top. Garnish to taste with spring onions and coriander (cilantro) and serve with a dip of chilli sauce.

Our Secret
If you are in a hurry, buy pre-prepared fresh chicken stock from the supermarket and dilute it to taste. To give the stock an extra kick add a drop of sesame oil, red wine vinegar and a pinch of pepper just at the last minute and serve the soup with a small plate of chilli sauce. Everybody's taste in stock differs and many will need to add soy sauce at the table to increase the savouriness.

Invigorating Chicken Soup

Chicken is thought to be good for the functions of the stomach and spleen. And certainly it is the easiest on the digestion and the natural choice for convalescence. But this soup has a special herb, radix astragali or huang qi, designed to invigorate the body by gently strengthening its yang aspect, its qi and the spleen itself. Most Cantonese supermarkets will sell huang qi; it looks like long, tough flat splints of wood.

Soak the mushrooms in hot water for 30 minutes, remove the hard stalks and slice the caps. Reserve the soaking water. Tie the *huang qi* together with a piece of fine string.

Heat the oil in the wok over a high heat, swirling the oil around. Scatter in the ginger, turn and then add the chicken and mushroom. Coat the chicken in oil and turn until it all changes colour without browning. Add the bamboo shoots, soy sauce, *Shaoxing* wine and salt and coat thoroughly.

Transfer the contents of the wok to a casserole and add the soaking liquid from the *huang qi* and mushrooms with 1 litre/2¾ pints/4 cups water to the casserole. Place the bundle of *huang qi* in the pan. Bring to the boil. Skim off any froth. Cover and simmer gently for about 40 minutes.

Remove the *huang qi* bundle. Move the chicken to one side of the casserole and slide the fensi down the side to the bottom. Add the Chinese cabbage, carefully keeping it to one side. Simmer gently for another 5 minutes. Scatter with spring onions.

Serves 10

6 Chinese dried mushrooms

100 g/3½ oz *radix astragali (huang qi)*, soaked for 20 minutes, soaking water reserved

1 tbsp vegetable oil

6 cm/2½ in piece fresh root ginger

1 kg/2¼ lb chicken drumsticks, halved

100 g/3½ oz bamboo shoots

2 tbsp dark soy sauce

3 tbsp *Shaoxing* (rice) wine or medium sherry

2 tsp salt

100 g/3½ oz fensi (glass) noodles, soaked in boiling water for a few minutes until just soft, then drained

½ small head Chinese cabbage, cut into 3 cm/ 1¼ in strips

2 spring onions (scallions), finely chopped

Our Secrets
You can make this soup in advance, adding the fensi and Chinese cabbage just before serving.

The good thing about this soup is that, unlike many Chinese medicinal herbs and substances, it tastes really good. But even better – it makes you feel wonderful! Do your friends a favour and make a great potful. We like to serve this after midnight at New Year, to fortify them for the future.

Cross the Bridge Noodles

Serves 2

60 g/2 oz lean beef, cut into thin slices then finely shredded

60 g/2 oz fresh plaice

60 g/2 oz fresh prawns (shrimp)

60 g/2 oz preserved cabbage (snow pickle), shredded

2 tsp *Shaoxing* (rice) wine

2 slices fresh root ginger, finely shredded

2 tsp light soy sauce

1 litre/1¾ pints/4 cups enhanced chicken or fish stock

pinch of salt

240 g/8 oz fresh egg noodles or white Shanghai noodles

30 g/1 oz young spinach, roughly chopped

2 tsp sesame oil

Pearl, one of the next generation in the clan and a true gourmet at heart, e-mailed us from Yunnan to tell us of her discovery of Cross the Bridge Noodle soup. This Yunnan soup was apparently dreamed up by the chef of a nobleman. This man's son repeatedly failed to pass the imperial examinations so his father shut him up in the garden studio in the middle of a pond for the duration of one winter. The only way out was across a bridge which linked the island to the main house. The family chef, wanting to deliver hot food to his unfortunate charge devised Cross the Bridge Noodles. He carried noodles and thinly sliced raw meat, fish and prawns on one dish, together with a bowl of hot broth covered with a thick layer of chicken fat all the way from the kitchen to the island studio. The single most important factor in the success this soup is the temperature and quality of the stock.

Using a very sharp knife (a fish filleting knife or a Chinese chopper if possible), slice the beef, fish and prawns (shrimp) as finely as possible, thinner than a matchstick. Mix them together with the preserved cabbage (snow pickle), *Shaoxing*, ginger and soy sauce and leave to marinate for 30 minutes.

Bring the stock to a rolling boil. Add a pinch of salt. Meanwhile, boil water in another pan and blanch the noodles and spinach together for about 30 seconds. Strain and arrange in the bottom of 2 large soup bowls. Arrange the seafood and meat on top.

Take the boiling stock from the stove and pour directly into the bowls. Dress with the sesame oil. Leave to stand for a couple of minutes to give the contents time to cook.

Our Secret

There are many different ways of serving this dish. Some chefs break a raw egg into the bowl. You can use any fish or meat so long as it is lean and cut to the finest slivers so that it cooks quickly. Place the bowls in a very hot oven so that they are burning hot and don't reduce the temperature of the stock. But remember to warn your guests!

Chicken and Sweetcorn Soup

Here is a thick creamy, fragrant soup that is a winner with everyone, especially children. It is very popular in Chinese restaurants in the West. Serve it as a starter or as a light lunch.

Marinate the chicken for 30 minutes in the egg white and salt.

Heat the wok and add the oil. When it is hot, scatter in the ginger and spring onions and turn in the oil. Add the chicken and stir fry for just a few seconds until the surface changes colour.

Add the wine and turn together. Immediately add the simmered stock, sweetcorn, soy sauce and cider vinegar and bring to the boil. Turn down the heat and add the rice or cornflour mixture and bring back to the boil.

Season with pepper and sesame oil. Garnish with radish and parsley and serve immediately.

Serves 4

240 g/8 oz/1 cup chicken breast, thinly sliced

½ egg white

pinch salt

2 tbsp vegetable oil

2 slices fresh root ginger, finely minced

2 spring onions (scallions), finely chopped

1 tbsp *Shaoxing* (rice) wine or medium sherry

450 ml/15 fl oz/scant 2 cups chicken stock, kept at a simmer

1 x 8 oz can creamed sweetcorn or sweetcorn, liquidised

2 tbsp light soy sauce

2 tsp cider vinegar

2 tsp ground rice powder or cornflour (cornstarch) dissolved in a little water

pinch white pepper

2 tsp sesame oil

flat leaf parsley and finely sliced radishes to garnish (optional)

Our Secret
We have purposely developed this recipe so that it has slices of chicken floating in bright thick corn yellow stock. Chinese don't liquidise soups, but this recipe does taste excellent smooth, mellowly sweet and creamy. Lo children have all been brought up on Chicken and Sweetcorn soup – so wholesome and easy to digest.

Index